Towns and Villages
OF ENGLAND

CRICKLADE

D1189023

DIANA HOLMES

ALAN SUTTON

First Published in the United Kingdom in 1993 by
Alan Sutton Publishing Ltd · Phoenix Mill · Far Thrupp · Stroud
Gloucestershire

First published in the United States of America in 1993 by
Alan Sutton Publishing Inc · 83 Washington Street · Dover · NH 03820

British Library Cataloguing in Publication Data. A catalogue record for this
book is available from the British Library.

Library of Congress Cataloging in Publication Data applied for.

Typeset in 11/13 Bembo.
Typesetting and origination by
Alan Sutton Publishing Limited.
Printed in Great Britain by
Hartnolls Ltd, Bodmin, Cornwall.

Contents

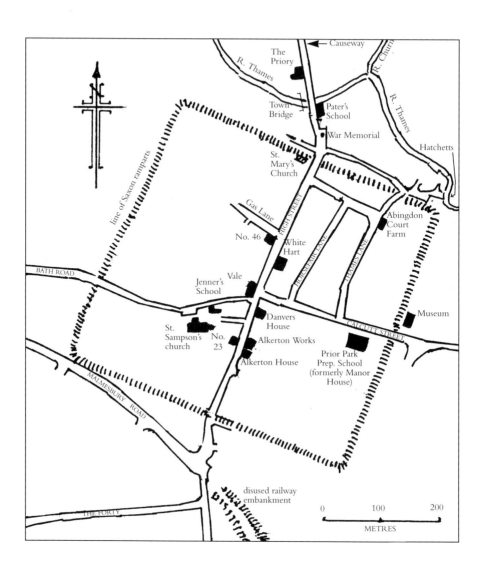

CHAPTER ONE

Beginnings – Romans, Saxons and Normans

The infinitely variable form of the English landscape means that there are almost always good reasons why a settlement which grew to even moderate size should have done so at that particular place. The geology of the area could be one – accessible stone for building, a plentiful water supply, gravelly (and therefore drier) land, or richer soil for growing crops for instance - or the reason could be geographical.

In the case of Cricklade the geological and geographical reasons were tempered with those of military necessity so, as is usually the case, the earliest settlement came about by a mixture of different influences. The overriding consideration, however, must have been that the site was at a place where an existing trackway crossed the river Thames and the pragmatic Roman surveyors, searching out the most practical route for the expansion northwards, would not have been slow to appreciate this.

At the time of the Roman invasion the Atrebates tribe occupied a large part of England south of the Thames. Like most of the Iron Age peoples they lived in villages of small thatched timber houses on land suitable for growing crops and pasturing animals; they used iron tools and had wheeled vehicles, horses and dogs. The Romans, moving westwards, built the town of Calleva (Silchester) in their territory. To the north the Dobunni occupied another large stretch of country extending as far as the middle reaches of the river Severn; their 'capital' was at Bagendon 3 miles north of Cirencester. The inter-tribal trackway ran between the two and must have been used by the Roman surveyors to guide them in planning a marching route north, a route which was later to form the line of one of their great roads in southern England - Ermin Street or, as some authorities will have it, Ermin Way.

A large part of Ermin Street is still in use almost 2,000 years later. Skirting Newbury at Speen, it makes its way over the Downs past the back of the M4 service station at Membury, descends the sharp hill into Wanborough, and joins Hyde Lane as it goes through Upper Stratton on the eastern edge of Swindon to the Turnpike roundabout on the A419 just south of Blunsdon. From the top of Blunsdon Hill the line continued to run in long straight sections with slightly angled bends at two points, one of 7 degrees just north of Cricklade and another, sharper one, near South Cerney airfield. Today the requirements of dual carriageway construction often blur the original line but it can be followed easily on the Ordnance Survey Landranger map. From the top of Blunsdon Hill today a fine view suddenly appears so that, on a clear day, miles of north Wiltshire's grassy farmland stretch out towards the gently rising slope of the oolitic limestone which forms the Cotswold Hills in the distance.

The Roman surveyors would have seen a rather different view. Immediately below the steep hill, itself composed of hard Coral Rag stone, was 3 miles of dense forest growing on the heavy clay soil. The trackway led

Taken during the floods of 1968, this photograph shows why the Romans chose to abandon the straight line of Ermin Street at Calcutt and divert it on to higher ground, the future site of Cricklade. Roman surveyors would have plotted the road from the top of Blunsdon hill in the background.

through this towards three low hills near the Thames, Common Hill, Eysey and Hailstone, all standing slightly above the surrounding land, which in winter would be marshy and susceptible to floods. Near and beyond the river the forest would be thinner where gravel underlay the surface, and a tongue of the Latton gravel deposits reached almost to the Thames.

Following their usual practice the surveyors would have used the elevation of Blunsdon Hill to align the next section of road crossing the river where the straight line dictated. This led them to the marshy wet area at Calcutt which within a short time they abandoned, no trace of a ford or bridge remaining. The practical Roman engineers, seeking a drier alternative, diverted the road first west and then northwards on to the slightly higher ground to arrive at the river crossing. This remained the route of Ermin Street (the modern A419) until 1975, when the town's bypass, constructed with the benefit of modern highway techniques, reverted to something akin to the original Roman route.

At the bottom of the gentle (High Street) slope was the point where the floodplain would be at its narrowest, a dry approach from either side being possible apart from a stretch of perhaps a quarter of a mile from the Thames where several small streams and one river, the Churn, flowed on their way to merge with the larger river a short distance downstream. It is an area which is still prone to flooding. Whether the Romans used boats and replaceable timber bridges to cross the water, or whether their engineers built the first version of the arched stone causeway which provided a permanent means of crossing, and which is still in use today, is not known, but the latter seems the most likely. The slight bend in the road referred to earlier occurs at Weaver's Bridge where the 'new' Roman route realigns itself with the original.

Although a good many finds of Roman origin, coins, fragments of pottery and jewellery, have been found in Cricklade it is not usually considered that there have been enough to signify a permanent settlement even though the articles came from different periods of the occupation. One possibility is that a marching camp was established where the forces of the future Emperor, Vespasian, could gather themselves and prepare for the next move northwards into the country of the Dobunni whose response to invasion was unknown, unlike the Atrebates who had been friendly. A position where they could defend the river crossing would seem ideal.

Later in the occupation, as *Corinium* (Cirencester) grew to be second only to *Londinium* in size, the river itself became important as a means of communication. The site of the river crossing coincided with the highest point of navigation on the Thames and it is likely that many cargoes destined for *Corinium* were unloaded here to complete the journey by road.

There are traces of two Roman villa farms nearby. Kingshill lies between the rivers Key and Ray on slightly raised ground, which later became the

Another 1968 picture showing why the Saxons chose Cricklade's dry site for their settlement; the floods come up as far as the tree-lined banks of the Thames. The High Street houses are of many periods but all adhere to the Saxon street line, most having their original burgage plot length of almost 200 feet.

common arable land of the Saxon town. The other, near Latton, is at Lertoll Well farm (Field Barn on some maps) but has not been properly excavated and is protected as a Scheduled Ancient Monument.

★ ★ ★

The 'blank' period in English history known as the Dark Ages followed on the withdrawal of the Roman forces from Britain in the middle of the fifth century. Traffic on Ermin Street diminished for there was no longer need for regular communication between, or reinforcement of, the towns, forts and other settlements established during the 400 years of Roman occupation. The likelihood is that the site near the river crossing was deserted.

The first 500 years yielded up only one event which some scholars have judged to have taken place at or near Cricklade – although even this is uncertain. Saint Augustine, the first Archbishop of Canterbury, had been sent by Pope Gregory I together with forty other monks to convert the Anglo-Saxons to Christianity and establish the authority of the Roman see in Britain. It was a successful mission, especially after word of the king's conversion and baptism had spread, and by 604, eight years after their landing in Kent, Christianity had taken hold sufficient for a meeting to be summoned with other bishops. This was said to have taken place 'at Augustine's Oak on the borders of Hwicce and the West Saxons' and there have been several theories as to where this might have been, but it is generally accepted that the meeting would have been nearby.

It was to be almost three centuries later before the country under the inspired leadership of Alfred the Great was to emerge as a united monarchy with judiciary and legislative bodies which provided the basis for sound government. The year before his accession as King of the West Saxons (Wessex) in 871 Alfred's army had won a battle against the Danish invaders at Ashdown, near Lambourn, a victory won largely by Alfred's bravery. The Danes were immensely strong and were determined to subdue the whole country, not being content with the extensive lands in the east, midlands and north which they already held. The Saxons had to fight many battles in the next few years until in 878 a decisive victory at Edington (near Westbury) gave some respite during which Alfred extended the territory he controlled by peaceful means. A final thrust by the Danes towards the end of his life (he died aged about 50) was also unsuccessful.

This then was the background to what was to become the most significant period in the development of 'the place by the river crossing' as the name Cricklade is freely translated. The ninth century, 1,100 years ago, seems remote to us today but the results of the Saxons' defensive building and town planning can be perceived clearly when walking around Cricklade and looking with informed eyes at the pattern of the streets and houses. It is a satisfying study, for the town has been called 'the most intact example of a late Saxon new town in Britain'. How did it come about?

Sensible of the threat posed by the Danes coming from their kingdom of Mercia to the north of Wessex, Alfred established a string of forts and fortified towns which became boroughs. Some were already in existence and others were founded to supplement them. Malmesbury, Cricklade and Oxford were intended to be strategic fortresses with an immediately available local garrison. Cricklade, where the main road from Wessex to the north crossed the Thames, was an obvious place to defend, for any invading army taking that route would of necessity have to pass through to make further progress.

It seems likely that the causeway (whether or not it had been built by the Romans to endure for the intervening centuries) would have been in a state of decay and extensive repairs, or even an entirely new construction, would have been necessary. A seventeenth-century piece of doggerel speaks of the existence of twelve arches and most of these can still be traced, some still being in use in times of flood.

The defensive town wall which the Saxons built has disappeared. Excavations by several teams of archaeologists show that it consisted of a scraped up clay bank between 20 and 30 feet wide, reveted by an ashlar-faced stone wall 5 feet thick. The stone came from Blunsdon Hill and was later removed piecemeal as useful building material when the original timber houses were replaced. The soft, level ground made it comparatively simple to divert some of the smaller watercourses to form part of the defensive system. From the documentary evidence of the Burghal Hideage it seems that the periphery of the walls, set in a square, measured no less than 2,036 yards. Responsibility for garrison duty was laid down as four men per rod (pole or perch = $16\frac{1}{2}$ feet) of wall, that is about 1,500 men, although a goodly part of this complement was assigned to neighbouring settlements from where they could be summoned at short notice.

Once the fortifications were constructed it was necessary to establish a settlement within to provide a population for their defence, and it is highly probable that in the fortresses of this period settlers were encouraged by the king to take up plots on easy terms as his tenants. The planned town which was built is reflected in the present arrangement of streets to a gridiron pattern. The High Street has two parallel side streets, Horsefair Lane and Thames Lane to the east, and the remains of a back lane on the west side. Ermin Street entered from the east although it is not altogether clear how, or how far, this continued past the High Street; another cross lane was later to become Gas Lane. There was a central market-place and gates in the middle of the four walls.

The High Street, then as now, was by far the most important of the streets and was where most of the houses were situated. Allotted on the burgage system, unique to tenure in ancient boroughs, the rented plots conformed to a regular pattern. Most frontages were of 2 poles (33 feet) although some, mainly at the highest part of the street furthest from the river, were double in size; several of the larger houses in the town were later to be built here.

Walking down the street today many, but by no means all, of the frontages of the shops and houses still conform to these dimensions. Then, each standard sized plot had a long garden of 12 poles (66 yards), while the houses were constructed of wood and thatch, crudely built and dark inside. The side lanes would have held the storehouses, granaries, smithies and workshops essential for the community's existence. The south-west quarter of the town

This aerial view taken in 1947 shows clearly the Saxon street plan of the town with the back lanes parallel to the High Street. Since the 1950s new housing has filled up much of the area on the south and west side of the town. The railway track, curving westwards, was lifted in 1964. Approximate north is to the right of the picture.

seems to have been allotted to the church for here were also the parsonage, tithe barn and glebe land later to become Parsonage Farm.

There were still considerable areas within the walls which were not filled with houses. There was plenty of space to divide up into hurdled paddocks for plough oxen, cattle and horses, if not for safety then for convenience. It has been estimated that more than 120 burgages were let, which might suppose a population of around seven hundred. There must have been bakers, butchers, shoemakers and certainly ale houses to provide for them.

Most agricultural activity took place outside the walls on land which was held by the borough. Arable cultivation was on that slightly higher land between the rivers Ray and Key on which the Romans had sited their villa-farm at Kingshill. A good mile from the town gates the approach would have been either from Ermin Street, using the east gate, or from the road going

This snowy scene was photographed about 1880 and is a rarity in that it shows the remnant of the old back lane, which ran parallel to the west side of the upper High Street. The roof of number 23 can just be seen on the right. Houses built since now cover much of the open space.

south from Cricklade. Here, two bridle paths (still existing), one from the Dance Common and the other leaving the Hayes Knoll road after a further half mile, led to the arable fields. The names of the farms in this triangle indicate their ancient origins – Ox House, Headlands and Farfield.

Two large meadows, the North Mead (North Meadow) and the South Mead provided hay and pasturage; nearer the town the Hitching would have been used for vegetables and bush fruit. To the west the boundary of Bradon Forest came as far as the Fiddle, almost up to the town walls. Although a royal forest the people of Cricklade gradually encroached on the woodland and as it was cleared of timber for fuel and building material the open spaces created more pannage for their pigs and grazing for their few cattle.

Each burgher paid a rent of one or two shillings a year to the lord and this was collected by his reeve. The rent included, besides the house and garden, defined strips in the town arable and stints of grazing on the town meadows, a stint being the allocated number of cattle allowed on the grazing. He also had the use of the borough commonage and of the town mill. In addition he had the very valuable right to sell all or any part of his burgage holding.

This right was used to great effect in very early times by those who sought to buy up the arable strips of fellow burghers, later holders buying up complete burgages. Gradually a large farm with considerable pasturage rights came into existence and this was the origin of the Manor of Abingdon Court, which came to be referred to as being subservient to the Manor of the Hundred and Borough of Cricklade. The new landlords' power over their tenants in directing them how to vote in elections became a decisive influence when the Borough first gained the right to send two burgesses to represent them in Parliament in 1275, and no doubt contributed to the sorry history of electoral corruption in the town which continued for over 800 years.

The rights which each burgage holder received in return for his rent were concomitant with the duties he was expected to fulfil. These were largely connected with the defence of the town, repairing the wall, manning his appointed sector in times of emergency, maintaining the bridge, causeway and streets and taking his turn in various offices when appointed by the King's reeve. Today two relics of this system of burghal tenure remain; there is still a Lord of the Hundred and Boro' and, following the Enclosure Act when the remaining town land was allotted, the right of burgage holders to pasture on North Meadow was preserved.

There are, however, other tangible reminders of the age in the shape of coins from the Cricklade mint. More than sixty have been found, three being in the possession of the Cricklade Historical Society. Others are in museums in this country and, as a result of subsequent Danish pillaging and the demands of the Danegeld, many are in Scandinavia. Alfred's grandson, King Athelstan, decreed in 928 that there should be one coinage throughout the land, a silver penny of 240 per pound by value and weight. All the fortified boroughs were to have their own mint and Cricklade's was one of the earliest, established about the year 979; the last coin discovered has been dated around 1096.

★ ★ ★

The coming of the Normans probably made little difference to Cricklade and its inhabitants. The country seemed to be settling down and the town's defensive role became less important. The feudal system which continued throughout the mediaeval period had become widespread as the king rewarded his knights with land. The Domesday Book shows that a good many of the burgages had been amalgamated, for it records that 'the Church of St. Peter, Westminster, holds the Church of Cricklade and has there many burgesses and a third penny of that vill'.

There was, however, to be yet another wave of warlike activity during the miserable 'nineteen winters' known as the Anarchy in the reign of the last Norman king, Stephen. One William Peverel of Dover built an illegal wooden castle in a place described as being surrounded on all sides by water and marshes, a site never since identified. A supporter of the Empress Matilda, a claimant to the succession, he is said to have made himself a nuisance to the surrounding district. Matilda, however, had apparently been shown kindness by the people of Cricklade whilst fleeing the king's forces in this nasty civil war. A disastrous expedition in 1147 by her teenage son, the future Henry II, involved his sailing from France with mercenary troops for an attack on Cricklade, which failed. Short of money, he was forced to beg for Stephen's mercy appealing to him as a kinsman and asking for money to return home. Stephen, glad to be both chivalrous and rid of the boy, obliged him.

Perhaps it was the 'kindness' that had been offered his mother which later led a more mature Henry to grant an unusual Charter when he visited the town in 1155, enjoining that 'the men of Cricklade be quit of toll or passage money and of all other customary dues . . . wherever they shall come throughout my whole land'. One of the three witnesses was his Chancellor, Thomas à Becket. This right was renewed by successive monarchs up to James I when, regrettably, Crickladians had to start to pay the various dues which they had hitherto been excused.

A few years earlier the anonymous author of the *Gesta Stephani* described Cricklade as being 'in lovely surroundings, abounding in all kinds of riches'. Today the first part of that nice description, '*in loco delicioso*', is the town motto.

CHAPTER TWO

Seven Centuries Pass By . . .

Cricklade's role for the first thousand years of its existence had been essentially a defensive one, its inhabitants providing a force to repel those who would seek to control the river crossing or breach the frontier between Wessex and Mercia. King Alfred's victories over the invading Danes and his subsequent setting up of judicial and legislative systems which formed the basis for effective government of a single kingdom, denied Cricklade the function which gave it being. Never again would it be a frontier town of military significance. Like hundreds of other places in England it became a small town inhabited by people engaged in the many trades which were required to serve the needs of those who lived in and around it. And, apart from epidemics of disease or an occasional day's excitement, that is how matters remained for many centuries.

Cultivation of the land continued on the open field system using crude implements, wooden ploughs being pulled by oxen since horses were too valuable to be used as draught animals. The field crops were wheat, rye, oats and beans but the generous size of the gardens belonging to the Cricklade holdings allowed the burgesses to rear poultry, and often a pig, as well as growing vegetables and fruit trees.

The houses were usually single storey, timber framed with wattle and daub infilling, most roofs usually being thatched. Some were of two storeys, such as 46 High Street, and for others the householders had utilized stone taken from the town walls to build some of the more substantial properties. Water came from wells and there was no drainage other than a wide ditch on either side of the street which took the slops and ordure towards the river.

By the 1500s the appearance of the countryside had begun to change and holdings began to be amalgamated to form small individual farms enclosed by fences or hedges little seen in north Wiltshire before. There were more cattle and the local cheese was in demand. Bradon forest was encroached upon more and more for pannage for pigs and timber for fuel and building. Sheep, the source of the wealth of the nearby Cotswolds, had become common. Farming became more remunerative, and the old mediaeval system was breaking up.

An unforgettable day for those who witnessed it must have been September 1st, 1592 when Queen Elizabeth I, together with all her court,

The tower of St. Sampson's church not surprisingly became known as 'the glory of North Wiltshire'. Completed only forty years before Elizabeth I's royal progress through three counties in 1592, those in the huge cavalcade must have seen it from miles away.

passed through on one of the last of her great royal progresses. The huge procession had left Lydiard Tregoze, where she had knighted her host Mr. St. John, and was bound for Down Ampney House where she was to spend the night as the guest of Sir John Hungerford. The numbers who came to see their Queen must have been several times the normal population of the town for word of her journey would have spread far. The Market Hall, standing on its ten columns, had been built only twenty-three years before by Sir John's grandfather, another Sir John, and was the most prominent structure in the town. It must have made an excellent vantage point on that extraordinary day.

John Aubrey, the Wiltshire antiquarian, was travelling in north Wiltshire a little earlier but formed an exceptionally jaundiced view of its inhabitants who, he said:

> only milk the cowes and make cheese. They feed mainly on milke meates, which cools their braines too much, and hurts their inventions. These circumstances make them melancholy, contemplative and malicious . . . their persons are generally plump and feggy: gallipot eyes, and some black: but they are generally handsome enough.

The Town Cross stood in the central market area of the High Street until it was removed to St. Sampson's churchyard. The White Swan inn stood on the corner of the narrow Bath road with the half-timbered and jettied White Horse, later to be rebuilt and become The Vale, opposite.

An early Lord of the Manor, Baldwin de Reviers, was first granted the right to hold markets and fairs in the town in 1257 but these seem to have been suspended during the period of the Black Death and after later smallpox epidemics. They were held in the open in the wide High Street until the Market Hall was built in front of the White Hart in 1569. By 1720 there was a weekly market on Saturdays and four additional fairs during the year one of which was special to the goods of the chapmen, the itinerant pedlars on whom rural people depended for so many small but essential goods.

The weekly markets lapsed once again (probably following a severe smallpox outbreak in 1783) but in 1837 a Market Committee was formed to revive them on a monthly basis, an advertisement in the *Wilts. and Gloucestershire Standard* inviting attendance at the 'First Monthly Great Cattle and Corn Market Toll-Free'. The committee also introduced fat stock shows which survive today as the Cricklade Show held on the August Bank Holiday. Horse sales had been conducted in Horsefair Lane for centuries. Markets continued to be held in the High Street on the third Tuesday of each month until 1944 when they were moved to the railway station yard at the request of the military authorities; they were finally abandoned in 1953.

The Civil War seems largely to have passed Cricklade by apart from a September day in 1643 when the Parliamentarian army was returning from

Market Day was the third Tuesday in the month and cattle were sold in the High Street, the auctioneer moving on between lots: here he is in front of the White Horse. The former White Swan inn had become a wheelwright's, Clark Brothers; the Medical Hall was burnt down in 1895.

Gloucester. One of their number, Serjeant Foster, kept a diary, which records under the 16th:

> We advanced from Cicester five miles to a village called Letton, where our London Brigade was quartered that night; the Lord Generall, with his Army quartered a mile further out at a Market-towne in Wiltshire called Cricklet; at the village aforesaid were ten cartload of Cavaliers, who were sick and lame, and brought thither to be quartered, who when they heard we were marching to this place, they then found their leggs and run away; this day we had a wet march, and in the night a false alarm. Sabbath day, September 17, we marched from Cricklet to a Market-towne called Swindowne, 8 miles.

Another Market Day scene, but taken some twenty or thirty years later, for an early motor vehicle is in the middle of the street and the White Hart (just above the car) has been rebuilt.

In 1643 a number of the Parliamentary army spent a night at 'Cricklet' and may have kept their horses in the Paul's Croft field. Photographed before 1896, the cottages, builder's yard and broken down shed (with a tree growing through the roof) were later demolished.

On the 18th there was a skirmish near Aldbourne, followed on the 20th by the battle of Newbury. A single spur of the period found at the entrance to Paul's Croft field is the only relic which provides a clue to where the horses may have spent the night.

Parish records, especially those dealing with the relief of the poor, provide a picture of what life in the town for the sick and indigent must have been like. Entries in the St. Sampson's Overseers record book for 1800 show travellers passing through the town to be hastened on their way with a measure of charity:

> Sailors as called at church – 2s.6d.
> The black man around the town and promising to leave – 6d.
> Black man in distress for Liverpool – 6d.
> Gave a woman with 3 children all the small pox upon them to get them along - 2s. 6d.

Although it was twenty-seven years since a bad epidemic affected the town smallpox remained a menacing disease. Edward Jenner, a Gloucestershire physician, first tried out a vaccine in 1796 but a further two years went by before his findings were published. The Cricklade apothecary, Dr. Kinneir, one of several members of the same family to be doctors or lawyers in the town, must have seen the worth of Jenner's discovery early, for in 1801 he was paid £13 15s. 0d. for the innoculation of 265 people at 1s. a head. The town's other doctor, William Wells, was paid £7 17s. 6d. as his yearly salary for attending to the residents of the workhouse. This was in the old Jenner school building, which cannot have been a very salubrious place for an entry in 1803 shows 'Man paid for killing ratts in workhouse - 5s. 0d.'

The Enclosure Acts at the end of the eighteenth century finally saw the end of the mediaeval town field system; in turn this led to depopulation and poverty in the countryside. At Cricklade the remaining parts of the town's arable land and the South Meadow were enclosed under an act of 1796 to be followed by another in 1814 affecting the open ground of Common Hill. William Cobbett, the essayist, on his great journey through the southern counties of England in 1821 (later recorded in *Rural Rides*) wrote a description of Cricklade which has become much quoted although it should perhaps be seen in the context of the general depression he found throughout his tour:

> I passed through that villainous hole Cricklade about two hours ago, and certainly a more rascally looking place I never set my eyes on. The labourers look very poor; dwellings little better than pigbeds and their food nearly equal to that of a pig. This Wiltshire is a horrible county.

Cobbett, a remarkable, self-taught man, was an expert in Parliamentary matters, for in 1803 he had begun publishing his 'Parliamentary Debates' which subsequently passed into the hands of Mr. Hansard. Cobbett's opinion may well have been coloured by an awareness of Cricklade's unfortunate reputation in electoral matters. Combined with the gloom that can be engendered by a miserable late autumn afternoon (the date was November 7th) it was perhaps enough to set a reasonable man against a place!

It is no exaggeration to say that Cricklade was notorious throughout the country for the corruption of its elections and its electorate which, even for the times, was remarkable for its depth and extent. The borough first sent two burgesses to represent it at Parliament in 1275 and this continued even though the town stayed much the same size whilst others, much larger, remained unrepresented. Such places with a disproportionately small electorate became known as 'rotten boroughs' and were ripe for the picking by predatory political adventurers not averse to bribery and cheating to achieve their ambition to become an MP, with the pecuniary advantages which went with the office. These practices were at their worst towards the end of the eighteenth century. The account of the way in which they were conducted reads today like something from Gilbert and Sullivan generously spiced with malice, rather than serious participation in the constitutional processes of the country.

Elections were held in public and since 1695 they had usually been held in the Widhill aisle of St. Sampson's church over a period of five days. After the close of poll each day the participants and their supporters adjourned to one or other of the town's inns to plan how their votes could be further enhanced. In 1774, at a meeting at the White Swan, the town bailiff, who acted as returning officer, agreed to close the poll as soon as a particular candidate was ahead. By dint of an opponent having his ear to a chink in the ceiling this was overheard and the plot misfired, but the consequences rumbled on for months until the matter was finally settled by a Parliamentary committee.

The borough's boundaries had gradually extended beyond the town walls and a dispute involving the voting rights of the householders in seven small cottages in Calcutt Street similarly dragged on. In some parts of the town the original tenement gardens had been infilled with small properties into which were planted complaisant voters.

The Cricklade scene was enlivened in the 1780 election by the candidature of Paul Benfield, who had returned to England after some years in India. Originally an engineer skilled in building fortifications he made his fortune by banking and trading, lending some Indian princelings considerable sums of money. His cousin, Crook Godby, the landlord of the White Horse, arranged with the bellringers that each time Benfield visited the town they were to ring a peal, and this piece of showmanship, combined with his local connections and limitless money quickly ensured he became the favourite candidate.

In order to obtain the necessary qualifications Benfield had bought property in the town (and with it their occupants' votes) and was negotiating for the purchase of the town's manor. Jonathan White, one of the agents he employed, was notoriously corrupt (and therefore greatly esteemed by the Cricklade electors) and informed them of what they were to expect not by the crude cash-in-hand methods used by his opponent but by assuring them that 'all was right' and tapping the ground with his stick a certain number of times. The Cricklade electors understood this language perfectly and that each tap meant a guinea! All the public houses with the exception of the Swan, his opponent's headquarters, were ordered to keep open house.

Benfield, a handsome looking nabob who was caricatured by Gilray as 'Count Roupee', was successful in the election but promptly returned to Madras afterwards, where, together with his fellow Cricklade MP, John MacPherson, he engaged in some most unsavoury financial dealings. He returned to England in 1788, lost his money through speculation and died impoverished in Paris in 1810. MacPherson's election had been ensured by the shabby and illegal activities of Lord Porchester whose agent, the landlord of the White Swan, handed out £5 for each promised vote. The King's Head and the White Horse were also used as election headquarters.

Samuel Petrie was the only participant at this time to seem even faintly 'clean' but his candidature never progressed far and he was never preferred by the Cricklade electorate, who were far too inured in the corrupt culture they had long known. He did, however, set about bringing some of the corruption to light in a long and complicated series of law cases during which the judge had to reprimand many of the Cricklade witnesses for lying, being drunk or having very poor memories!

The importance of the manipulation of property holdings (and thus voting rights) became clear in the 1812 election when Joseph Pitt was one of the candidates. Pitt was a lawyer and a property speculator who developed estates in the part of Cheltenham that became known as Pittville, including building the graceful Pump Room which was intended to rival that of Bath. Unlike many of the candidates put before the Cricklade voters, Pitt had already ensured himself a firm foothold in the town by the purchase of the manor of Chelworth and of scores of small properties, especially those which had been recently inserted into burgage gardens. Three years later he purchased the manor of the hundred and borough of Cricklade, thus for the first time combining the manors of Chelworth and Cricklade under one owner.

Landgrabber that Pitt was he was declared to be 'of the strictest honour' in his private life, praise which may have carried the implication that he was not quite so correct in his business dealings. He remained MP until 1831 but eventually had to sell the Cricklade estate to meet heavy debts.

Although the constituency had been enlarged in 1782 the anomaly of its representation by two members continued until the Redistribution Act of 1885. This created the new division of North Wiltshire and together with the introduction of the secret ballot in 1872 at last did away with the practices which had given Cricklade such a bad name for so long.

Soon after the ending of the Crimean War in 1856 some unusual mementoes of the conflict were given to the town. Two huge cannon, last fired at Sebastopol, arrived at Minety station to be duly hauled to Cricklade by teams of white horses. Legend says there were forty of them, but a proper account of the event, or the name of the donor who made such a grand gesture, are absent. The guns were real enough, however, and stood outside Brook House at the bottom of the High Street, where they somewhat inappropriately flanked the war memorial until they were removed to meet an ignominious end in the Second World War, when they were melted down for scrap.

The town's war memorial, built after the First World War, outside the walls of Brook House was flanked, somewhat inappropriately, by two Crimean war cannon. They met an ignominious end in the Second World War when they were sent for scrap.

These children coming out of Bath road may have been on their way home from Jenner's school. The Jubilee clock was erected in 1897 and has suffered several mishaps through traffic, the elaborate finial being knocked off in the last war.

It seems that the population of the town altered very little for many centuries. No accurate figures exist before the first official census in 1801 when there were 1,330 inhabitants; a hundred years earlier the estimated figure was 1,100. In 1841 it topped 2,000 for the first time, but dropped back in subsequent census' and by 1951 was still only 1,881. Since then the explosion of new development and the creation of several large residential estates has radically changed the situation, the 1981 population figure being 3,727.

CHAPTER THREE

Churches and Chapels

The proudly handsome tower of St. Sampson's, Cricklade's parish church, stands out like a beacon in the predominantly flat landscape which surrounds the town. From a distance it often seems to catch the sunlight, inviting approach, so it is little wonder that it has long been known as 'the glory of North Wiltshire'. The tower, though magnificent and almost of cathedral-like dimensions, is somewhat out of proportion with the rest of the church but no less to be admired for that. Chronologically it is at the end rather than the beginning of the church's story.

The Saxons chose the site, the highest point in the town, for their church which was built of stone. This was probably brought to the town at a time when the revetting of the defensive walls was being carried out to strengthen them against the Danes. The first written reference to the church at Cricklade dates from about 983 when one Aethelmaer left it £1. Two fragments of pre-Conquest stone carving are embedded in the porch wall above the massive door.

The church and the land with which it was endowed were given by Edward the Confessor to his favourite, Robert Fitz-Wimarc, the Staller. Robert died before the Domesday Book was compiled, but later charters issued by William I (the Conqueror) confirm that the mother church and lands at 'Crikkelade' had been given to the Abbey church at Westminster. At the time they were worth 'a third penny', about £5, so it was a fairly profitable property. The church was still in the holding of the Abbey a century later, but by 1202 it had passed out of its hands.

The dedication to St. Sampson is a most unusual one shared with only a few other churches. St. Sampson lived in the sixth century, and although some sources say he was Welsh, others that he was half Breton, much of his life was spent in Cornwall where there are several other St. Sampson dedications. He founded the Abbey-Bishopric of Dol in Brittany and the dedication at Cricklade may have been at the behest of that half-Breton, Robert Fitz-Wimarc.

The reference to the mother church is interesting for it meant that it headed a group of at least nine dependent 'lesser' churches in nearby villages extending from Somerford as far as Purton, as well as several small chapels or

St. Sampson's tower stands like a beacon in the landscape, and this drawing by J. Buckler, from around 1810, shows how its almost cathedral-like proportions tend to dominate the rest of the church.

'field churches' including St. Helen's chapel on Hailstone (Holy Stone) hill. They would all be served by a collegium of priests, who would have lived in a house immediately to the west of the church on what was to become Parsonage Farm.

There are indications that the Abbey rebuilt the church about 1180. Outside it is easy to see that the two side aisles were added to the older nave at different times, the stone of the nave's west wall having a distinctive pinky-brown tone quite different from the grey of the remainder; the bottom courses of stone in this wall are amongst the oldest parts of the church. Both side aisles were added in the middle years of the thirteenth century, the nave wall of the south aisle having some very early carved stones, including two fine Norman animals, high up above the arcade; there has been speculation that one of the others is a Roman altar stone. The chancel was remodelled a century later. Viewed as a whole the interior of the church shows a typical mix of mediaeval architectural styles and periods, overshadowed, it must be said, by the sheer impact of the tower.

This soars up from the central crossing to a high lantern vault. The ornamentation on the columns and ribbed vaulting above is astonishing in its variety and number — shields, crests, canopied niches and crosses abound;

there are sixty-five bosses. Outside, the openwork battlemented top and plump pinnacles top off the whole to complete this 'glory' which took more than fifty years to build.

The heraldic decorations on the shields and rib bosses provide numerous clues as to who it was provided the motivation – and the money – for such a monumental work. Several of them bear the arms of various members of the Hungerford family, the lords of the Down Ampney estate 2 miles north of Cricklade. Enormously rich from their extensive land holdings in the south and west of the country, in Wiltshire, Gloucestershire, Berkshire, Oxford and Somerset, they were by far the biggest landowners in the district. They had both power and influence in Cricklade, and later on, following the dissolution of the monasteries, bought more land, closer to the town, from the Crown.

The other family closely identified with the tower is that of John Dudley, Duke of Northumberland, whose involvement occurred many years after the start of the building work. Masons' marks, unique to each craftsman, show there was a pause in the construction, which had started in the early years of the sixteenth century; it is very possible the money ran out. In 1547 Dudley was created Earl of Warwick and two years later acquired from the Crown the manors of Calcutt and Chelworth Parva (both just outside the town) for his son, John, who was about to marry Ann, daughter of the Lord Protector Somerset. In 1551 he was created Duke of Northumberland and, ambitious as ever, he married another son, Guilford, to Lady Jane Grey.

Perhaps it was on a visit to his son John that Northumberland heard of the unfinished tower and saw it as an opportunity to satisfy his vanity (and gratify further his overweening ambition) by paying for its completion. This included the carving of many armorial badges to which strictly speaking he had no right and prominently, and rather surprisingly, the four 'pips' of playing cards (spade, heart, diamond and club) which William Morris once suggested might commemorate a gambling success that produced the funds for the building.

Alas for Northumberland, it did not save him from the consequences of his overriding ambition for, having attempted to instal his unfortunate daughter-in-law as monarch, he was punished by being beheaded in the Tower of London in 1553 shortly after the accession of Mary Tudor. His legacy is St. Sampson's tower.

There are, however, other interesting things to see in the church. The wide north aisle to the left as you enter forms the Widhill Chapel, Widhill then being a distant part of the parish, now in Blunsdon. Until 1864 it was shut off from the rest of the church by an oak screen within which sat the children during the service and the lengthy sermons of the time. This part of the

St. Sampson's from the Bath road about 1882. In front is the Stoneyard (now the church car park) where the Cricklade Waylands stored the materials for road repairs. In living memory men were employed to do nothing but break down large rocks into small chippings using long hammers.

This delightful pastoral scene has disappeared for ever, the pond at Parsonage Farm filled in and the site covered by flats and housing.

church also fulfilled a civil function as it was used as an early polling station in Parliamentary elections. The headless effigy of a woman on the recessed fifteenth-century tomb in the wall was retrieved from the churchyard, but was so worn that she has never been identified for certain.

Near the altar a table tomb topped in gleaming black marble is that of Robert Jenner of Widhill, a City of London goldsmith and MP for Cricklade for twenty years. Jenner died in 1651 and his philanthropic legacies are spelled out in detail on his tomb, Cricklade benefiting by the money to build a free school in the parish and 'twentie poundes a yeare for the maintenance of it forever'. The school, built in the year following Jenner's death, backed on to the churchyard and must have been one of the earliest in the district, but unfortunately the endowment was insufficient and it fell into disrepair. From 1726 until 1824 it was used as a poorhouse, but reverted to a school in 1840, remaining so until 1959. Today the handsome building with its mullioned windows serves as the Parish Hall.

The Hungerford Chapel on the opposite side of the church, to the right of the chancel, was built by Sir Edmund Hungerford who died in 1484, but its fabric could not counter the thrust of the new tower and a flying buttress had to be added as an additional support. Several fine pavement stones in the chapel and in the adjoining choir vestry commemorate members of the

Pleydell family who lived in Alkerton House (then called Pleydells) in the High Street. Edward, an MP for Cricklade, lies alongside his wife Arabella but her stone records more the distinction of her father than her own virtues; he was 'Chancellor of ye Exchequer and Privie Counsellr In the Reigns of King Charles 2nd King James King Willm. Queen Mary'.

Nearby lies Edward's spinster sister, Mrs. Martha Pleydell, who died in 1727, the title 'Mrs.' being given to elderly unmarried ladies during this period; she gave 'twenty Shillings per Annum for ever to ye poor of this Town and Branch for Candlles in this Church'. The 'Branch' is the fine chandelier which hangs in the chancel today. A poignant verse on a stone in the Hungerford Chapel records the death of the infant daughter of a nephew, Richard, and his wife Elizabeth. The child, Betty, died in 1736 aged 5 years and 22 weeks:

> My friends and parents do not weep,
> I am not dead but gone to sleep.
> I from this world am gone to rest,
> God takes him who he loves best.

Towards the back of the church in the south aisle is the old church clock which used to be mounted in the belfry, its tenor bell sounding out the hours to the townspeople for several centuries. Built in 1658 by Richard Hewse of Wootton Bassett, it had the newly invented 'anchor' escapement added in 1670 but was removed from the tower in 1937 when a blacksmith's forge was taken up in an attempt to repair one of the bells. It was rebuilt, as nearly as could be ascertained in its 1670 form, in 1970 – and still works. All the wheels are of wrought iron and two of the stone weights have Norman tooling on them.

The church, like many others, underwent heavy restoration in the Victorian era and although, seemingly, much needed to be done, much else was lost in the process. The work took place in 1864 and a later Vicar left a notebook giving a vivid picture of what it was like to attend St. Sampson's prior to the restorations 'gathered from the account of those who knew it then'. Here is a quotation from it:

At the W. end of the Church were three galleries, the largest in the centre, stretching across the whole Nave – In this gallery were the organ and there sat a choir of men and women. In former times an orchestra, consisting of a flute, violin, and bassoon occupied this gallery – they were at one time assisted in leading the music of the service by a lady with a strong and piercing voice. On each side of this main gallery, in the aisles, was another gallery, containing appropriated pews.

The Widhill Chapel was surrounded by an oak screen, which at the time of the restoration was considered so dilapidated as to be past renewal and was therefore removed. Immediately before the restoration the children sat in the north transept, but previously they sat in the Widhill Chapel. During the service Mr. Wiltshire, the schoolmaster, might have been seen walking about the Chapel with a cane in his hand, admonishing such children as were unruly with a firm hand.

Up to the time of the restoration the children attended St. Mary's in the morning. The Rector being given to long sermons, it was not unknown for the boys – or some of them – to escape attendance at St. Mary's as they proceeded down the Street, by way of Gas Lane. In the afternoon the children attended St. Sampson's where the sermon of the Vicar was not so long.

The nave was filled with high oak pews of all shapes and sizes and facing all manner of ways, each being allotted to a particular family. Some were heated by their own stoves, the smoke from which caused considerable problems. An

The house now called Candletree used to be St. Sampson's vicarage. Taken about 1890 this shows the vicar, the Reverend Henry Morton, with his wife. The churchyard gate is seen across the Bath road.

The school founded by Robert Jenner in 1652 stands alongside St. Sampson's churchyard; the adjoining headmaster's house was added later. The Town Cross is to the right of it. The cottage by the gate at the end of Church Lane has a plaque on it, 'Circa 1490'.

unfortunate fire in 1823 started suspiciously near the pew of the town's High Bailiff, Dr. Taylor, whose daughters were later to commemorate him by the gift of the east window.

One can only wonder if the destruction of the 'dilapidated' oak screen was necessary and the loss of the oak pews must be regretted for the pitch pine pews which replaced them can only be said to be typical of their time. A later Vicar of high church persuasion had the choir stalls painted crimson and traces can still be seen as the not very attractive sludge-coloured over-painting rubs away. The floor was formerly stone flagged but red and black tiles replaced this, and it was channelled for heating pipes covered with metal grilles. The galleries were taken down, as was a metal screen dividing the chancel from the sanctuary. Whilst the work was being done services took place in the (then new) Town Hall, with order being restored in time for Christmas.

★ ★ ★

At the bottom end of the High Street the small but beautiful church of St. Mary's is a complete contrast to its larger sister. No one seems sure which church was the first to be built in the town, for although what we see of St. Mary's today is basically Norman, there are unmistakable signs that an

This watercolour of St. Mary's church was painted early in the last century. The dormer windows in the roof lit a gallery which was reached by a staircase entered by the door to the left of the base of the cross; both were removed in the restorations of 1862.

earlier small chapel existed here. The tiny north chapel, rather awkwardly joined at a 10 degree angle to the chancel, points to this for it stands just inside the line of the Saxon town wall and would have been close to the north gate of the town; indeed it may even have been built on the site of the gatehouse.

From the street the church has a somewhat homely air, much less grand than St. Sampson's, with the smooth lawn in front contrasting with the shady, wilder old graveyard beyond. Both building and lawn are raised higher than street level and the fine fourteenth-century cross, complete with all the sculpture in a four-sided tabernacle head, stands high not far from the pavement. The mediaeval builders of the rather stumpy thirteenth-century tower may have intended it to be higher but, perhaps without a Northumberland to pay for it, work stopped and was never resumed.

Inside, the eye is immediately drawn to the fine, richly carved chancel arch, a splendid example of Norman work dating from between 1120 and 1150. The rest of the church was originally built only a little later but there has been much rebuilding since and the inevitable Victorian restoration in 1862 when the unsightly and rickety gallery which disfigured the interior was

The rector, the Reverend Hugh Allen and his wife stand outside the restored church, dormers and staircase now gone, after 1862 and before 1882 when Mr. Allen died. To increase the natural light inside new dormers were installed in 1908.

removed. This was reached by an outside staircase and was lit by two dormer windows which were removed, only to be replaced in 1908.

The additional light benefits the church greatly and shows up the quality and depth of carving on the Jacobean pulpit (possibly part of a two or three decker) and the wide oak cornices which line each aisle. The rectangular oak altar table, dated 1727, was made in Charles I's time and was perhaps fortunate to survive the destruction wrought in the years of the Commonwealth which followed soon afterwards.

The clock, usually a reliable timekeeper, has its face in the gable of the nave overlooking the High Street, but its works are right back in the tower, the two being connected by an ingenious rotating rod carried under the ridge of the nave roof; it was presented by Major Henry Smyth in memory of his wife in 1863. Earlier timekeeping had been reliant on an 1822 scratch sundial, also facing the street, which replaced an earlier one.

Cricklade was divided into two parishes, St. Sampson's with a vicar and St. Mary's which had a rector, until 1952 when they were united. At the same time Latton-cum-Eysey was added to the joint benefice, but remains a separate parish. St. Mary's, only 121 acres in size, was the smallest in the Bristol diocese, the southern boundary being Gas Lane. Church registers exist from 1683 and the first has the word ABRACADABRA written on the inside cover, suggested to be a charm against the plague.

The little church was declared redundant in the 1970s but a happy solution was eventually reached. Since 1984 it has been leased back to the local Roman Catholic congregation who care for it and worship there and, as Cricklade is an ecumenical parish, are joined by members of the other churches in the town several times a year.

★ ★ ★

Beyond St. Mary's and over the Thames bridge stands a house, the Georgian front of which belies its ancient origins. Together with some of the adjoining properties it is on the site of the Priory Hospital of St. John the Baptist, founded as a guest house for poor wayfarers some time before 1231. Outside the town walls but close to the causeway section of Ermin Street, it was perfectly placed to provide sustenance for any indigent travellers who passed by.

The interior of St. Mary's is small but full of good things; unfortunately they seem to obscure each other on this old postcard. The fine early eighteenth-century brass chandelier half hides the dog-toothed Norman arch, and the lectern stands in front of the Jacobean pulpit.

The Priory provides the background to this undated photograph showing the Town Band leading a parade of the Cricklade Working Mens Society, many of the men wearing chains or badges of office. The Band, an institution very much alive in Cricklade today, came into existence in 1872.

Founded by Warin, one of Henry III's chaplains, he and all subsequent wardens were granted the right to collect timber and brushwood from Bradon Forest for the use of the poor and the brethren, the forest then being quite close to the town. The objects of the founder were modified in 1415 when the Bishop of Salisbury decreed that the needs of poor priests, unable through age or infirmity to carry out their duties, should be the prime concern of the foundation, and that only so far as its means allowed should it continue to give rest and refreshment to poor travellers.

Henry VIII's dissolution of the monasteries ended its charitable work and in 1550 the whole property, excepting only the valuable bells and lead roof, was sold to William Fontayne and Richard Mayne. The building has, of course, changed completely but the outline of the original east window can still be picked out in the stonework of the gable end nearest the road. For a period in the late eighteenth century the building served as the poor house for St. Mary's parish, but for the last 200 years it has been privately owned, at one time by the owners of the fellmongering and tannery business whose activities took place by the river close by.

★ ★ ★

The baptismal ceremonies held periodically at Hatchetts ford on the edge of the town continued into this century and drew crowds of townspeople to witness them; this photograph shows the last to be held by the Particular Baptist congregation. The town museum now occupies their old chapel.

Non-conformism reached the town in the eighteenth century, but of the four chapels which were built only one is still fulfilling the role for which it was intended. The present United Reformed church in Calcutt Street was founded in 1799 as a Congregational chapel, the original front being replaced with a new face in 1878. Of the Methodist chapels both the Wesleyan, by the Town Bridge, and the Primitive Methodist chapel are used for other purposes.

The fourth chapel was built in 1852 for the Particular Baptists, a strict sect believing in predestination and who, having found no biblical evidence for the baptism of infants, held to the belief that such a sacrament should only be administered to adult believers. The chapel lacking a baptistry, the ceremony took place in the open air at Hatchetts ford on the Thames near Abingdon Court Farm, normally a place used for little else but watering the cattle.

The pool by Hatchetts was deep enough for the purpose and the banks gentle enough to accomodate the crowds of townspeople who came to watch the unusual event. On the day of baptism the female candidates wore cream flannel dresses and the men black silk cord suits. After the immersion, which was total, face upwards, the newly baptised sat in broughams, one for each sex, to drain and when the carriage was full it departed to deliver its soaking passengers home.

The church kept up its numbers in the town, maintaining its own pastor, until the First World War, but afterwards numbers declined and it was closed in 1937. The tombstones of many of the early members of the church rest against the wall of the garden in front of the simple, stone building which is now the town's museum, run by the Cricklade Historical Society. This welcomes visitors either during its regular opening hours or by prior arrangement.

CHAPTER FOUR

The Thames and the Canals

The importance of the Thames in Cricklade's early days has been made clear in the first chapter of this book. The river rises at Thames Head in Trewsbury Mead only 9 miles to the north near the village of Coates, where a spring, which nowadays frequently dries up in the summer, emerges. Until 1974 a recumbent statue of Father Thames marked the place but this is now at St. John's Lock, Lechlade, the highest lock on the river, where it can be more easily seen and perhaps better looked after.

The river flows as a gentle stream west of Somerford Keynes and then through Ashton Keynes, where it runs in a cheerful babble alongside the High Road through the village, crossed by numerous small bridges leading to the attractive stone houses on the other side. Soon after Ashton a substantial stream, the Swill Brook, joins it from the west, but it is not until Cricklade that several other rivers and streams combine to make the Thames a river practicable for any kind of navigation – and that for only very small craft.

The wide floodplain of the upper Thames round here is fairly flat, with Hailstone Hill the only feature to stand out with any prominence. From Somerford it is nearly all gravel bearing land and many of the hedged dairy pastures which were here have disappeared to be replaced by water. As the gravel diggings are exhausted they fill and, retitled as 'lakes', they become part of the recreational area known as the Cotswold Water Park. However, since many are still company owned the use to which they are put varies greatly; whilst some have been allowed to become unkempt and are of somewhat desolate appearance, others have been landscaped with banks and trees to make them of positive environmental advantage.

The many clubs and other organisations which lease or own the lakes offer a variety of leisure pastimes – sailing, wind surfing, water skiing, jet skiing and fishing of different kinds. In the Somerford vicinity some lakes, left deliberately wild, are valued by ornithologists who come to see the huge numbers of migratory birds which visit.

The Water Park has been in existence since 1967 and was intended to be a recreational attraction for people from places up to one and a half hours' drive away – potentially millions of visitors. However, as many of the lakes offering sporting activities are used by private clubs there are limited opportunities for casual visitors to join in, only a few small car parks and little refreshment other than that obtainable from the village pubs. The ordered development of the Park has probably not been helped by its position sitting astride the county boundary between Wiltshire and Gloucestershire, as well as that of two District Councils. To get four local authorities to agree on policies as diverse as mineral abstraction, tourism development and the protection of the environment, let alone safeguard the interests and welfare of the local people, continues to present difficulties.

Cricklade, however, has hardly been affected by the Park, near as it is to it, but it is still affected by its old enemy, winter flooding, which can cover large areas, particularly those near the Thames both above and below the town. The flooding has apparently decreased in recent years although whether this is due to the efforts of the Thames drainage engineers or the creation of so many water-filled gravel pits upstream, we do not know, but according to the recollections of Cricklade people recorded fifty years ago the floods were much worse and lasted longer during the last century.

A large tributary, the Churn, comes into the Thames at Cricklade and indeed there are many people who say its source, at Seven Springs high up on the Cotswolds above Cheltenham, should rightly be called the source of the Thames for the Churn is indeed very much longer. An entirely different river in character, the Churn runs down a particularly beautiful valley to Cirencester where it divides to make its way through the town, emerging to flow through South Cerney and Cerney Wick before reaching the north side of Cricklade's North Meadow, the Thames forming the southern boundary.

The right to navigation on the Thames as far as Cricklade has existed since the middle ages but it has never been exercised without difficulties, often due to its shallowness and, in summer, sheer lack of water. There were other problems, however, and in 1677 thirty-four inhabitants of Cricklade drew up a petition and sent it to the town's two Parliamentary burgesses asking that the hitherto 'free and undisturbed passage for smaller boats and barges . . . advantageous to ye said town in furthering the trade thereof' should be maintained. 'Now of late the said boats have been stopped and interupted att a certain place called St. John Bridge by one Captain Cutler and not permitted to pase upon the said river without the payment of a considerable sum of money for severall [i.e. each] boat so passing.'

Nowadays the right to navigation is more theoretical than practical for the river has substantially altered. Downstream from the town it once flowed quite slowly through water meadows not very different from those still at Inglesham, but modern land drainage and the earlier removal of old weirs has resulted in long stretches with almost vertical banks between 5 and 10 feet higher than the summer water level. Had the river been a useable waterway when the Thames and Severn canal was constructed in the 1780s the builders would hardly have excavated the final 10-mile stretch from Cricklade to Inglesham.

From the day the canal opened the river suffered almost total neglect, and even after the establishment of the Thames Conservancy in 1866 little was done. Almost thirty years later a petition to the Conservancy pleading for the maintenance of a minimum depth of 12 inches of water up to the Town Bridge was met with an acknowledgement of liability – but a plea of poverty.

In the mid-1980s a group of keen boaters, encouraged by the Inland Waterways Association, proposed a scheme whereby the channel would be dredged to the depth of a metre, the bends straightened out and the banks reinforced with netting to permit motor boats to reach Cricklade. To the relief of many, and in the face of considerable opposition from riparian owners and environmental groups, it all came to nothing – including the suggestion that Cricklade should once again have its own wharf for the benefit of river traffic, which seemed unjustified and impractical on financial grounds alone.

An early photograph showing the lower end of the High Street known as the Knoll. The wharf, which extended as far as the gates of Brook House (behind the large tree), had been filled in years before. The rector of St. Mary's and his wife stand on the left whilst customers wait at the door of the Red Lion.

The wharf had existed from Roman times until the 1830s when it was abandoned and filled in. At first the Romans may have found the sloping gravelly banks made the pulling up of their barges easy, later building a wharf for the unloading of goods for *Corinium*. The Saxon town certainly needed a wharf and records show that barges were still using it as late as 1828 when they navigated up to West Mill. It extended along the High Street in front of the row of cottages on the west side as far as Brook House and the war memorial, almost up to the line of the Saxon town walls.

At the bottom of the High Street the Town Bridge has been recognised as the limit of navigation rights since the middle ages. In the eighteenth century contemporary title deeds show it as being quite narrow and it probably had a raisable platform to allow barges through. It was rebuilt in 1854 by the feoffees (trustees) of the Waylands Estate with an arch which always seems too small to take the fast flowing stream that in winter rushes down the deep willow-lined channel; it has somewhat scornfully been termed 'the dam with a hole in it'. At that time stone steps led down to the river and a semicircular grille prevented children who had gone to draw water from being pulled in.

The Town Mill was a few yards upstream from the bridge on the site of the house which now stands between the river and an ancient drainage ditch called the Stank. A mill was a necessity for a settlement of any size and the

The Town Bridge, known irreverently as 'the dam with the hole in it', was rebuilt by the Waylands feoffees in 1854. In winter it is hardly adequate for flood conditions, but this picture must have been taken in a very dry summer when Mr. C.T. Cuss, a feoffee (trustee) could stand in the river bed.

Willows now line the banks by Town Bridge, but in this turn-of-the-century picture the interest is on the chestnut tree, now doubled in size and a notable feature of this end of the town. The arch on the right side of the bridge used to lead to steps for the use of those who came to draw water.

Saxons must have established one soon after the foundation of the Borough. Centuries later the lowering of the water table and the consequent loss of power led to its abandonment, its function being taken over by West Mill and the windmill on Common Hill.

By the eighteenth century the mill buildings had changed their purpose from grinding corn to fellmongering and tanning, the water and oak bark from Bradon Forest both being essential for the latter. There were lime pits and a fleshing shop where the skins were washed, and it is hardly surprising that later the Thames Conservators made strong protests about the effluent and consequent pollution of the river. Some of the skins produced supplied the glove makers, a traditional trade in the town first mentioned in 1590 and still surviving today.

All traces of the town's other mill, West Mill, have disappeared in a housing development. The earliest mention of it was in 1300 and it was to outlast by far the Town Mill, as it was operating until the end of the last century. The

The miller's cottage is dwarfed by the size of the West Mill buildings in this photograph taken about 1925. It must have been a hot summer for the bed of the Thames is dry; the normal level would have been up to the sluice on the left.

buildings fell out of use but the miller's house was still occupied in the 1930s before the Thames Conservancy Board demolished them all in 1938.

Towards the end of the eighteenth century canal building became the rage all over England. Whilst the carriage of goods by water had great advantages over the alternatives, pack horses or the even slower waggons using the poor roads, the rivers were by no means ideal. Apart from anything else their use entailed incessant quarrels between bargees and mill owners over the rights of navigation: letting one vessel through a flash lock often meant so great a loss of water that the miller was unable to grind his corn until the level built up again, which at times of low flow could mean several days.

With the beginning of the industrial revolution there was an urgent need for a better transport system, and once the Duke of Bridgwater had proved

West Mill lane was a pleasant rural backwater between the wars with the North Wilts. Canal cut alongside it. The miller's cottage was demolished in 1938 and the thatched cottage is long gone. New housing developments have infilled the fields between here and Cricklade.

what efficiencies and economies had resulted from the construction of his canal near Manchester in 1761 there was a rush to emulate him. Forty years on a complex system of canals had been built, most of them enjoying a comparatively short but prosperous life until the coming of the railways in the 1830s with their wider penetration and superior speed.

The idea of making a coast to coast link across the country had first been put forward by speculators in the reign of Elizabeth I, but nothing had ever come of the suggestions which proposed a variety of routes. However, in 1783 things moved fast and plans for what was by contemporary standards an enormous scheme to link the river Severn with the Thames got off the ground amazingly quickly. Three weeks after a meeting of the promoters three-quarters of the capital had been raised, the necessary bill passing through Parliament in April. In June construction of the Thames and Severn Canal began at the western end where the new cut was to link with the existing Stroudwater Canal. Not only was the 3,817-yard Sapperton tunnel to be the longest in England, and a source of wonder and amazement, but the project was the greatest civil engineering work to be carried out in Britain at that time.

The canal opened throughout in November 1789 and from the beginning found the supply of water a problem. At the summit level a six-sailed windmill drew up water from the Thames Head springs but only five years after the opening it had to be replaced by a Boulton and Watt steam engine. Lower down, the Churn was used to increase levels. A further difficulty was the impediment to navigation caused by the neglect of the Thames Commissioners, a very disorganised body at that time, in maintaining the river below Inglesham. This navigational bottleneck was overcome in 1819 by the completion of the North Wilts. Canal from Latton to Swindon eventually

Latton wharf at the northern end of the causeway was Cricklade's link to the Thames and Severn Canal. The core of the unusual wharf house, pictured in 1947, was a four roomed cottage, but the enveloping wings on three sides acted as a warehouse.

The front of the wharf house originally faced the canal, since filled in, but nowadays looks towards the Cricklade bypass. It presented its back (see other picture) to Ermin Street. Intended to house the canal's agents, a similar one was built at Kempsford.

joining the Wilts. and Berks., in effect bypassing the last 10 miles of the Thames and Severn.

Cricklade, therefore, had two canals within half a mile, able to transport heavy goods of which coal was by far the most important. The Thames and Severn, having never strayed far from the Churn all the way from Cirencester, turned away to the east at Weavers Bridge (the northern end of the causeway) where the agent's depot, Latton Wharf, was built. Both Latton and Kempsford had similar oddly designed warehouse buildings where a four roomed house rose between enveloping wings that served as warehouses; stone built, they were faced with plaster and stucco and topped by a triangular pediment. The house, showing its back to the old causeway road out of Cricklade and its front to the modern bypass (the canal in front having been filled in) is still there.

In the early days of the canal there was a considerable trade in grain from Lechlade, Cricklade and Cirencester to Bristol. In the other direction coal came down from Staffordshire and the Forest of Dean, the trade accounting for the large number of coal merchants that nineteenth-century directories record as living in Cricklade. Other merchandise included bricks, slates, salt, flour, malt, iron and timber.

By 1834 fly boats were running between Gloucester and London, providing a fast and regular service and using the water of the Gloucester and Berkeley and the Wilts. and Berks.; that year the number of boats passing the summit level was 1618.

The North Wilts. Canal opened in 1819 and had twelve locks in the 9 miles from Swindon, crossing the Thames on a small aqueduct at the north end of the North Meadow. The junction with the Thames and Severn was made at Latton Basin where another aqueduct once carried the canal over the Churn. The remains of the large basin, where cargoes often had to be reloaded due to the different dimensions of the barges the two canals used, are still there. Brick built and edged with huge dressed stone slabs it can be found down the track by the side of Street Farm, Latton. The contrast between the activity which once must have taken place there with the quiet and almost deserted condition it is in today is marked. The lock keeper's house has been much enlarged and altered but as a site of local industrial archaeology the Basin is well worth visiting.

A rare photograph of Latton Basin filled with water but with no sign of canal traffic. The Thames and Severn and the North Wilts. canals joined here and goods were transhipped from the T & S trows to barges suitable for work on the North Wilts., seen entering at the far end.

The convergence of the Thames and Severn and the North Wilts. canals within a few yards of the river Churn near Latton Basin necessitated the building of these distinctive bridges, removed since the war. Mr. E.J. Buttar painted this attractive picture in 1920.

Chelworth wharf on the Fiddle, a short distance north of its junction with the Forty, was the staging post for Cricklade traffic and Pigot's *Directory of Wiltshire* in 1830 advertised George Franklin's fly boats leaving three times a week to London, Abingdon, Oxford, Stroud and Gloucester.

Sadly it was not to last. All waterways, particularly those in the south and west, suffered with the coming of the railways, and the opening of the GWR line between Kemble and Stroud in 1841 saw canal company takings fall drastically. It was the beginning of a very prolonged end. The next sixty years saw several schemes to keep the company solvent, but in 1901 Gloucestershire County Council took over the management hoping that it would serve as a public asset and require only a small contribution from the rates. Unfortunately much more money was required to put the canal in order and the last boat able to pass through the whole length made the trip in 1911; commercial life had ended long before. The Thames and Severn was finally abandoned in 1927 although stretches of it, including one at Latton, had been used for pleasure boating for some years. The land and buildings were subsequently sold off.

The wharf which served Cricklade on the North Wilts. Canal was on the Fiddle at Chelworth, a little way north of the Forty. In the distance is the portal to the short tunnel under Horsey Down. The lane has now been built up and houses cover the field on the right.

A revival of a kind, albeit one not foreseen by the original builders, might yet be in sight. Canals having been successfully restored in other parts of the country the Cotswold Canals Trust have taken up the challenge of the Thames and Severn. So far considerable progress has been made in the vicinity of Stroud but, other than rebuilding the lock at Cerney Wick, little has yet been achieved east of the Sapperton tunnel. The problems posed by ensuring an adequate water supply, crossing the trunk road at Latton and obtaining the willing co-operation of landowners are formidable, but the Trust's hope of reviving this cross country water link may well come about if they can be solved. If they do, we may yet see the superstructure of pleasure boats making their way through the familiar fields to join the network of England's inland waterways.

CHAPTER FIVE

Roads and Commons

A n ancient trackway between the territories of two large tribes, the Atrebates and the Dobunni, existed long before the Romans came and built their new highway of Ermin Street. It crossed the floodplain of the Thames, if not at Cricklade then very near it, possibly slightly to the west where it probably utilized a crossing below Hailstone Hill. Passing through South Cerney, mainly by lanes which still exist, it linked with the prehistoric Whiteway to continue north. After the new road to *Corinium* was built it must have been used less frequently.

The Romans chose their crossing place for the reasons of geography and military necessity outlined in the first chapter, and the subsequent settlement, whether a marching camp or occupied by people responsible for maintaining the crossing, was small. Cricklade, then, evolved to fulfil a specific purpose during the occupation in contrast to *Corinium*, only 7 miles away, which developed from being a military camp to a provincial capital with all the economic and trading advantages requiring a radial road system which largely still exists.

When Roman rule ended trade declined, *Corinium* shrank in size and the importance of some of the roads leading from it, such as Ermin Street, decreased. For well over a thousand years it was never again as busy and its condition progressively deteriorated. It was always of lesser importance than its namesake, an earlier Roman Ermine Street, which ran from Pevensey to Yorkshire via London.

The town of Cricklade developed directly from the Saxon determination to defend the river crossing of the Thames, which became the northern frontier of Wessex. Alfred the Great's chain of defensive strongholds gave it a crucial strategic position between Malmesbury and Oxford so that, in essence, it was a frontier town beyond which was Mercia and the land of the Hwicce. Its road links were to the south and west towards the heartland of Wessex rather than north and east.

Malmesbury was both a fortified town and a religious centre and the road to it followed the slight ridge which raised it above damp land. The way south pre-dated Alfred's time for it led to a nodal point of ancient trackways, Barbury Castle (near Liddington), from where it continued to Winchester

The rough road into Cricklade from Purton about 1870. After the railway was built in 1883 a bridge crossed the road just beyond the turnpike gates; the toll house, demolished in 1964, is on the right in front of the big tree.

and Southampton. Later this road largely fell into disuse as the road through Purton to Wootton Bassett, linking centres of population, took over its functions.

The roads (if they could be called such) remained in the same poor state for centuries, dusty, furrowed tracks in summer and quagmires in winter, sometimes wandering away from the original track to find an easier way to traverse. Goods were carried on pack horses and most people did not venture far from their town or village; travellers were those with business, for the church, for the King or for trade.

In common with all parishes the people of Cricklade were responsible for maintaining the roads in and around the town, so it must have been a boon when in the reign of Elizabeth I they were at least relieved of some of the financial burden. A charitable transfer of land and property led to the creation of the Cricklade Waylands whose eighteen feoffees (trustees) were to 'mayntaine sustaine and repayre the High Waies about the said Towne of Cricklade'. The feoffees remained responsible for the roads and bridges for over 300 years, a duty which they carried out, sometimes carelessly and at other times more conscientiously, until the Local Government Act of 1894 transferred responsibility to the new County and Rural District Councils.

The Bath road turnpike house was very small and stood at Culverhay cross before it was knocked down in 1968. The hounds being exercised were from the VWH (Cricklade) hunt kennels which moved to Cricklade in 1886. Joe Willis was in charge, Ted Goddard is on the right.

The Waylands had been established for only twenty-five years when the Queen herself passed through the town on her 1592 royal progress on her way to Down Ampney. The huge procession of over 1,000 horses and perhaps 200 carts had come from Lydiard Tregoze, so it approached by the 'old' southern route crossing Dance Common on a raised causeway which can still be seen. Since the records tell us that there was an excellent harvest in 1592 the weather might well have been fine that day as the lumbering cavalcade made its way towards the town, and one can imagine that the great tower of St. Sampson's, its masonry only forty years old, might have been shining like a beacon in the afternoon sunlight. Whatever improvements the feoffees had managed to make by then, the wear and tear of that day must have been considerable!

The condition of the roads throughout the country was variable, parishes being reluctant to spend money on them for the benefit of strangers. A more reliable method of maintaining them had to be devised and Parliament eventually authorised the establishment of Turnpike Trusts to erect gates and toll bars where passengers would be expected to pay to pass through. Needless to say the charges were most unpopular, but by 1770 about 15,000 miles of roads were under trusts and journeys not only became easier but also much faster.

Mr. W.J. Giles lived in the Bath road pikehouse for many years. This photograph of the cramped downstairs room is interesting for its details, from the fob watch hanging from the beam to the big cast-iron open range fireplace.

Before the construction of the Oxford to Bristol turnpike in 1787 westward-bound traffic had used the Forty, passing through Chelworth (and a road since obliterated by a wartime airfield) to Minety, a generally level route which avoided the awkward slope of Common Hill. The turnpike builders, however, eased the gradient and improved the track, which had hitherto only been used by farm carts and waggons going to the common fields or the windmill on the crest. Tolls were collected at the Pike house on Bath Road which, regrettably, was demolished as recently as 1967 in the same 'clearance' that saw the end of the nearby fourteenth-century tithe barn. The other survivor of Cricklade's four pike houses, on the road south near the Forty, was knocked down the following year.

The increase in traffic and the number of travellers greatly benefited the inns of the town, the White Hart and the White Horse (its name was later

The Bath road approach to Cricklade has changed greatly only comparatively recently. This picture from 1909 shows the ancient tithe barn (said to date from the fourteenth century) which was demolished in 1967 to the regret of many townspeople.

changed to the Vale) being the busiest. The larger carriages and stage coaches found access to the former's yard obstructed by the Market Hall which had been built in front of it in 1569, and the Town Cross at the main crossroads similarly impeded entry into the narrow Bath road. Progress, however, could not be denied, and sometime between 1812 and 1820 both were duly removed, the ten columns on which the hall had stood being rescued to provide support for a cattle byre just outside the town; the columns are still there. The Town Cross is now in the churchyard.

The turnpike roads with their better surfaces and regular maintenance had greatly improved the lot of travellers but now another threat appeared to add to the perils of a journey. Highwaymen were not a new phenomenon, and had been a hazard of travel as far back as the 1300s, but eighteenth-century England was notorious throughout Europe for this particular crime. Provided travellers handed over money or jewels with the minimum of fuss little harm usually came to them, but these 'Knights of the Road', as they were euphemistically called, did not hesitate to shoot if carriages refused to stop or their guards put up a fight.

One of the most notorious to operate in Wiltshire was William Peare, one of a family of blacksmiths who lived at the Three Horseshoes. In 1782, when in his 20s, and in gaol for robbing the Chippenham mail, he escaped from

The main crossroads in Cricklade in the mid-1890s, only a cart by the narrow entrance to the Bath road in sight. The Portwell pump on the pavement in the foreground disappeared one night in mysterious circumstances!

Looking south from near St. Mary's church, this early photograph was taken in the late 1860s. The single-storey building on the right, now Blackwells taxi and tyre business, was a blacksmith's smithy; beyond the next house was a slaughter house.

Gloucester Castle and embarked upon a series of impudent robberies. A few months later he and a confederate were surprised whilst digging their way through a party wall between an empty house and one of the Stroud banks. Peare fled before he could be captured but his companion informed on him and directed the pursuers to Peare's father's house at 58 High Street, where he was found hiding in an ingeniously constructed roof space.

A general favourite among his comrades he went to the scaffold at Salisbury with dignity, carrying a nosegay and paying particular attention to the adjustment of the cord. His body was taken to Chippenham and suspended on a gibbet as a warning to others. Two months afterwards, after a day when several of his Cricklade friends had been seen in the town, it mysteriously disappeared; it is said to have been buried secretly near his home.

Minor roads remained the responsibility of the parishes and their maintenance was often the subject of local disputes. The ancient road from Chelworth over Hailstone Hill had become little used, but in 1847 the courts awarded damages of £685 8s. 9d. against the parishioners of Cricklade St. Sampson's for failing to maintain Hailstone Lane as an 'ancient common Queen's Pack and Prime Way'. It was a huge sum at the time and the claimant, George Newmarch of Woodwards Farm (now Hailstone Farm), must have felt he had won a major victory, if only for himself and for the benefit of a very few other people.

Horses continued to provide the motive power for both people and goods until the 1880s, when two new forms of transport changed the lives of many of the people of Cricklade. The railway arrived in 1883 to take people to Swindon or Cirencester so much more quickly and easily as well as opening up more distant horizons and opportunities both for work and for leisure. Nearer home the development of that simple machine, the bicycle, enlarged the scope of social life and courtship.

Motor cars arrived in the early years of this century and Cricklade had its first garage when Mr. L.O. Hammond, who had been chauffeur to Mr. Butt-Miller, the Master of the VWH (Cricklade) hunt, opened a motor shop at 100 High Street, repairs being carried out at the rear. Told to remove petrol pumps from the pavement outside, he later moved to larger premises in Calcutt Street where he employed over twenty men, expanding to run taxi and coach services as well as the garage.

The second half of the twentieth century has seen the re-emergence of Ermin Street once more to dominate the traffic flows around the town. The growth of private motoring after the Second World War meant the High Street, with its awkward corner, clogged up almost completely on holiday Saturdays and at other busy times. The closure of the narrow entrance to the Bath road and the diversion of traffic down a new road (which followed the

The postmaster, Mr. Harry Stephens, was about to leave Church Lane and take his youngest son, Jack, and his granddaughter, Phyllis Cuss, to visit his brother at Pinehurst for lunch when this photograph was taken in 1909. Phyllis, now Mrs. Hammond of Latton, remembers 'gramp's frock-smock' from his earlier days as a baker. The pony's name was Daisy.

Mr. L.O. Hammond opened a shop in 1912 selling bicycles and necessities for the new motor cars which he also repaired. The business grew and later moved to larger premises in Calcutt Street. Mr. Hammond (left) stands with Oliver Ashley in front of the original shop at 100 High Street.

Until the late 1920s Ermin Street crossed the Thames and Severn Canal at Latton on a steep hump-backed bridge, but after the closure of the waterway the road was levelled and almost all traces of its existence have disappeared.

The advent of 'high wheelers' in the 1870s and '80s opened up fresh horizons for young men such as Mr. Little. 'Safety bicycles', with wheels of equal size, superseded the high wheelers in the 1890s.

A peaceful scene around 1920 as the Bath and Malmesbury road left Cricklade. The VWH (Cricklade) hunt kennels at Keels can be seen on the left; they moved to Maisey Hampton in 1934. Doubledays field is on the right.

Local transport depended very much upon the horse until well into this century. This is the (men only) Bowls Club outing leaving from outside the Vale Hotel, which was kept by A. Edwards from 1915 to 1927.

line of the old railway track) together with the coming of the bypass in 1975 were greeted with great relief. The volume of traffic on the bypass, which links two major motorways, the M4 and M5, has increased immeasurably, but whilst it can still be heard in Cricklade at least it is no longer seen.

★ ★ ★

NORTH MEADOW AND THE OTHER COMMONS

At one time the town had several areas of common land in addition to Common Hill and the open fields of South Mead. Of them all only Dance Common and the North Meadow remain, the last a place now special to Cricklade which draws thousands to visit it each year.

The effects of the Enclosure Acts on the town were wide ranging but in one respect tidied up existing arrangements to put in place a reform which has lasted. The Act affecting the district was passed in 1814 and specified that the North Meadow (Normead) was to remain the property of the burgesses of Cricklade, an amending act passed the following year defining its use and administration. The system it laid down is still followed and has left the town with a 110-acre meadow which is famous for both its management regime and for the rare flowers that grow there.

The road up Common Hill in the 1930s, the Fiddle joining from the left. Until the Enclosure Act of 1814 the townspeople took their waggons and stock to the 212 acres of open common land around the hill.

The Domesday survey records the natural flood pastures around Cricklade and, before 1814, the people of the town had grazed their animals on the land for hundreds of years, the meadow benefiting from its occasional inundation in the winter months. Under the Act the land was redistributed so that each landowner had the same acreage, but in one piece rather than several smaller plots, thus making it easier to cut the hay crop. Marker stones defined the boundaries, and some of the older ones which remain still bear the initials of the original owners of that time. No fencing of individual plots occurred, an essential condition if the common grazing rights were to continue.

The meadow is Lammas Land, a type of common land where some or all of its benefits are enjoyed in common by a group of people who are not themselves the owners. From August 12th (Old Lammas Day) until the following February 12th certain inhabitants of the town have grazing rights, but for the rest of the year there are no common rights and the meadow is closed to animals to allow for the growth of the hay crop which belongs to the owners of the freehold.

Traditionally the Lord of the Hundred and Borough of Cricklade was responsible for the appointment of officials to oversee the management of matters on his behalf. This was coordinated through the Court Leet, a special kind of manorial court which still exists today. The Steward, the High Bailiff

This photograph of a vase full of picked fritillaries is many years old. Today, any picking of these protected flowers is frowned on and the North Meadow, the old Normead, has been a National Nature Reserve since 1973.

and Jurors appoint a Hayward whose duty it was to supervise the grazing of the meadow, ensuring only authorised stock was there and rounding up any strays. Nowadays the Hayward (the only one of the Court Leet officials to have a genuine duty) works closely with the staff of English Nature, which owns almost all the freehold. North Meadow is a National Nature Reserve having no less than 80 per cent of the British population of the rare Snakeshead Fritillary (*fritillaria meleagris*).

The little bell-shaped flowers hang down from a slender stem up to a foot high, having grown from a bulb. Most are purple, some are white and a very few red; all are speckled. Towards the end of April each year the meadow is a mecca for botanists who travel long distances to see these rarities. Wardens from English Nature try to encourage visitors to keep to the rights of way, but at least the picking of the flowers, quite common at one time, has ceased, and the vulnerable plants now receive a measure of the protection they deserve.

CHAPTER SIX

Cricklade's Railway

The single track railway which served Cricklade for eighty years, making its way across the Cotswold uplands and lush north Wiltshire farmland, was an important link in the chain of small lines which made it possible to travel across the grain of the already well-established main lines which radiated from London. For much of its existence it was concerned with purely local traffic but in both world wars the traffic on its lines multiplied, making its part in moving troops and supplies to and from the south coast ports of the utmost strategic importance.

In the period of 'Railway Mania' in the middle of the nineteenth century several schemes for linking Manchester and Southampton were put forward, two of them surveyed by Robert Stephenson. None succeeded, either through lack of finance or the opposition of the Great Western Railway, which remained an implacable foe of any upstart rival that sought to 'trespass' on what it regarded as its territory – the west of England.

The railway engineers persevered, and after the opening of several smaller lengths of line to the south the Swindon, Marlborough and Andover Railway Company was formed to complete the route to Southampton. The first part of the line from Swindon (Old) Town to Marlborough, opened in 1881 but was not connected to the main west country route more than a mile away in the New Town. After a legal tussle with the GWR the SMA were able to run their trains into Swindon station from the following February, albeit at a high 'ransom' fee for the use of the station which the new railway was only able to afford for a few years. The completed line between Swindon and Andover was opened with 'a sumptuous lunch' in early 1883.

In the meantime plans had gone forward for the next logical step, a northward extension of the line to Cheltenham where it would connect with trains running on the Midland Railway. The Act of Parliament to allow the new line had been passed in 1831, supported in the House of Lords by Earl Bathurst, who complained that he found it impossible to reach Scotland in a day; apparently the Midland express from Gloucester left a minute before the (GWR) Cirencester train arrived.

The first section of this new line to be constructed was that from Swindon to Cirencester, and this was completed in a surprisingly short time with stations at Blunsdon, Cricklade and South Cerney (for Ashton Keynes). The intransigence and financial demands of the GWR meant that passengers were unable to use Swindon main line station other than for interchange traffic and the connection of the new line, the Swindon and Cheltenham Extension Railway, with the SMA was to be at Rushey Platt, a mile west of Swindon station and then very much in the middle of nowhere.

The line was opened for goods traffic in November 1883 and, after the necessary inspection, was pronounced safe for passengers the following month, the inspection train covering the 16 miles between Cirencester and Swindon in twenty-two minutes. Celebrations at Cirencester had to wait until the New Year but on December 18th Cricklade welcomed the train with the Town Band playing 'A flower that bloometh' before a reception at

The Cirencester to Swindon section of the Midland and South Western Junction Railway opened in 1883. The lines seem to have been laid in this busy scene at Cricklade, but the traction engine and circular saw may have been cutting up sleepers for the siding line.

The haunches of the railway bridge where it crossed the Bath road must have required rebuilding early this century. Perhaps the little girls in their pinafores and hats had just come out of school.

the White Hart. There were sports, tea for the children and old people and a firework display. The next day the Vale of the White Horse hunt travelled by train to Swindon for the weekly meet at the southern end of its country.

The two small companies were amalgamated in 1884 to form the Midland and South Western Junction Railway. Financially things were in a parlous state and work on the further extension from Cirencester to Andoversford was at a standstill. However, the arrival of a new contractor and some refinancing in May 1888 saw the start of the formidable task of laying the track over land through the Cotswold hills with their many variations of gradient. Driving through the tunnel near Chedworth, where severe engineering difficulties were encountered, meant work continued by night as well as by day, 480 navvies being employed.

It proved impossible to continue the MSWJ into Cheltenham itself and the company's line ended at Andoversford, where it joined the track of the

Banbury and Cheltenham Direct Railway, to reach the centre of the town a few miles on. Through traffic began in May 1892 and included quantities of Burton beer for export and consumption in Portsmouth.

In the same year the company had a piece of good fortune in engaging as its General Manager Sam Fay, an energetic man far-sighted enough to see the possibilities of the new line. Fay's businesslike methods, collecting debts and station takings personally and implementing economies, virtually restored the company from bankruptcy. One measure was to increase revenue from advertisements on stations from such companies as W.H. Smith & Son. A locomotive, carriage and waggon works was established at the company's Cirencester station at Watermoor for the rolling stock, which was painted in crimson lake livery.

After seven years during which he transformed the company Fay left, much admired, later joining the Great Central Railway which he also revived, as it too had been almost bankrupt on his arrival. His success was recognised by a knighthood bestowed on him during a visit by King George V in 1912. In the First World War he became Director General of Movements and Railways; he died in 1935 at the age of 95.

The MSWJ, although on a reasonably sound footing, did not return much money to its long suffering investors. 1913 became its best year financially although the dividend declared was tiny and only received by the top-ranking shareholders. With the declaration of war in 1914 it became a vital artery in wartime communications and the volume of traffic carried for the following four years was staggering. Local people said 'them trains never stopped', loaded with wounded and soldiers on leave, often still covered with Flanders mud, who had crossed the Channel from Dieppe and Cherbourg and, going southwards, armaments and replacements of men and materials. The figures tell their own story; during the war the MSWJ carried 181,683 officers, 2,992,202 men, 134,852 horses and 5,730 cycles. 'Special' trains numbered 6,456 in addition to 1,488 ambulance trains; there were 9,021 ammunition trucks. In 1916 the mileage travelled on the MSWJ was 1,115,255.

After the war the traffic reduced to a level which once again made the railway no longer viable and in 1923 the MSWJ was absorbed by the GWR which, in its early days at least, had been such an uncooperative and unhelpful 'big brother'. Some of the drivers, remembering this, could not stomach working for the GWR and moved south to join the Southern Railway. The porters' uniform of green corduroy trousers, sleeve waistcoat, jacket and pill box hat was seen no more.

In the Second World War the line again played an important part in the war effort as a strategic route, although by then motorised movement of troops and materials was much more widespread. The line, single track for most of its length, often became jammed; during the Dunkirk evacuation seven trains were in Tidworth (on a short branch from Ludgershall) at one time. As in the First World War ambulance trains were numerous and at Cricklade, as in other places, jugs of tea would be handed up for the troops to drink as the trains made their slow, heavily laden, way through the station. In the opposite direction came war supplies and, in 1944, many thousands of troops being moved into position for D–Day.

Nationalisation of the railways in 1948 only prolonged the life of the line a few more years, for in 1961 passenger services were withdrawn from most sections, including that serving Cricklade, although the station remained open for parcels traffic (which included milk) for another two years. The last workmens' train from Swindon to Cirencester on September 8th carried a wreath fixed to the engine. The track from Cirencester to Andoversford was lifted in 1963 and the line through Cricklade the following year. It really was the end. The closure is often blamed on the radical cuts recommended by Dr. Beeching, then Chairman of British Railways, but in fact the die had been

This photograph of Cricklade station, taken from the north, shows the sidings behind the signal cabin. Staff and passengers crossed the line by the wooden walkway in the foreground.

cast well before, for the Beeching Report which caused the axing of so many rural lines was only published in 1965.

So much for the history of this modest rural line which must have opened up new horizons for many in the country villages it served, reliant before its coming on horse-powered transportation. Cricklade, a place of some size with a population around 1,800, generated a respectable amount of traffic, much of it connected with farming on the good pastureland of north Wiltshire. The variety can be shown by the facilities provided at the small station, which had a loop, four sidings, a goods shed, horse dock, cattle pens and a milk loading platform.

This last must have been the site of much activity for between eighty and a hundred churns a day had to be loaded into four vans on to the 6.50 pm milk train which made its way down the line to Andover collecting churns at most stations on the way, enough to fill seventeen vans in all. Each filled churn held 17 gallons. Arriving at Andover around 10 pm the engine, driver and guard

Cricklade station sometime between 1902 and 1912, the staff lined up to meet the train from Cirencester and South Cerney. Flower beds were always beautifully kept and edged with whitened stones.

would be changed and the milk sent on its way to Clapham Junction, Vauxhall and Waterloo. The greatest number of Cricklade loaded churns was 195 in one day in June 1923. The empty milk train returned from Andover at 12.15 am, occasionally, it is said, stopping for the crew to catch rabbits near Marlborough! Sorting out the churns, each with a brass plate with its owner's name on, kept the station porter busy along with his other jobs, meeting trains, filling and cleaning lamps and sheeting and roping wagons of hay and straw.

Blunsdon was also a busy 'milk station'. A good three miles away from its village the station stood on its own amidst dairy farms which provided the milk to fill sixty churns a day. Its importance, relative to passenger traffic, can be seen by the revenue in 1913: passengers £5, parcels (i.e. milk) £922, Goods £175. A platform was added at Moredon in 1913 for the collection of milk (twenty to twenty-five churns) which in itself gives an idea of the rural nature of the north-west side of Swindon at that time. The opening of the big Co-operative Wholesale Society creamery at Latton in the early 1930s put paid to much of this traffic, milk travelling there by road, and by 1935 the rail carriage of milk had decreased although some continued until the late 1940s.

Passenger services in the early days set out to accommodate all needs. Family saloons, invalid carriages or ladies only compartments could all be reserved, and in a part of England where hunting, racehorse breeding and, later, polo were important, special attention was paid to horse transport. The timetable stated: 'For the convenience of Gentlemen Hunting in the vicinity of the Line, Return Tickets for Horses will be issued at a reduced charge of One Fare and one-half at Owners Risk. The horses may return the same or following day.' Luncheon baskets were supplied at Swindon Town, and tea baskets, 6d. a piece, at Swindon and Marlborough.

There are many people in the town who, with a certain degree of affection, still remember the workmens' train which took them to Swindon each day. It left before 7 am to get the men (no one remembers any women using it) to the Town station by 7.30, most of them to work in the huge GWR railway works at the bottom of the hill. After the last war about twenty would make the journey daily returning to Cricklade after 6 pm.

The ordinary service was quite good, some six or more trains each way; at one time there was even a 'theatre train' from Swindon which arrived back about 11 pm. Before the war the return fare was 1s. 3d. The station was kept immaculate, the Stationmaster, Mr. Walkley, dressed in full uniform of thick navy serge with red piping whatever the weather. 'It keeps out the cold, keeps in the heat' he said. The rose beds, edged with split flints painted white, were his pride and joy. Near the station the road was so quiet that children played on it, the girls with hoops or whip and top, the boys waiting for an opportunity to jump on the next farmer's cart bearing its load of churns.

The signalman's telegraph provided unofficial contact with the outside world before telephones became common, and in the 1930s it was usual for Mrs. Delmege at the Manor House to send a servant down to the station to discover the name of the winner of the Derby.

A restoration society, the Swindon and Cricklade Railway Company, was formed in 1978 with the aim of relaying the line between Moredon and Cricklade. Progress, constrained by the lack of finance, has been slow, but a usable track now extends for a mile north of its base at the old Blunsdon station. Occasional steam and diesel trains run up the line, but the station itself (open most weekends) with its collection of railway memorabilia has become a site of interest to railway enthusiasts and other visitors.

Many of the car drivers commuting from Cirencester and Cricklade to Swindon and following, lemming-like, behind each other on the A419 during each morning and evening rush hour, might still remember the old line and regret its disappearance. Had it still been in existence it might have made the journey quicker, as comfortable – and a lot less stressful.

The embankment on the right-hand side of the bridge is now the only trace of the railway bridge crossing the Purton road. In this picture the toll house remains, but the gates have gone; the road has not yet been tarred.

CHAPTER SEVEN

Up – and Down – the High Street

Approaching Cricklade from the causeway with its several little bridges, the northern end of the town today looks hardly changed from the same scene one and quarter centuries ago. After the final hump of the High, or 'Blue', bridge the Priory abuts the road on the right, the outline of its original chapel window showing clearly in the stonework. Beyond it, and standing at a slight angle, is a detached house which stands on the site of the tanyard buildings that once took up the land between it and the river. In the middle of the last century it was a single-storey structure used by the Wesleyans for worship until they built a more substantial chapel on the other side of the road in 1870. Later it was used for glove making by the firm of Maslin and Ockwell (as well as having a printing press under the roof) before it was enlarged and became a private residence.

Past the chapel is an unmistakable Victorian school building, known to generations of Cricklade children as 'the bottom school'. Its correct name was Pater's School, after John Pater who founded it in 1860. Intended for infants it was extended fifty years later when the girls moved from Jenner's school, leaving that school for the boys' use alone. Jenner's must have been crowded before separation, for a year after, in 1911, the average number of girls attending Pater's was sixty-three, in addition to seventy-one infants. Co-education resumed again later.

The town wharf once reached past Knoll Cottage to just beyond the war memorial, the width of the road between the wharf and the row of old cottages opposite allowing enough space for the business of loading and unloading barges. This area, outside the town walls, was for centuries the place where the activities which might be described as industrial took place. Apart from the wharf and the tanyard, with its associated fellmongering and glove making, there was in the mid-1800s an iron foundry – its owner, William Chesterman, living at Knoll Cottage. The town's war memorial to the fallen of both world wars stands outside the wall of Brook House, which once belonged to the Buckland family, owners of another tannery to the rear of the house.

From here, as the street curves to the right and straightens, rising on its gentle slope, you are *intra mures*, or within the walls of the Saxon burgh. St. Mary's church would have been just within, at the north gate of the town,

68

This building near the Priory served as a meeting place for the Wesleyan Methodists until their own chapel was built in 1870. Used as a glove factory for years it has been enlarged and is now a substantial private house, but has lost its unusual windows.

and the wall would have continued through what is now the garden of the Red Lion public house.

It is probable that every house which is on an original Saxon house site in Cricklade's wide High Street has been rebuilt from four to seven times; today the frontages display a rich mix of building styles. The result is far from homogeneous but perhaps is more typical of a workaday local community than some of the architecturally more perfect (and historically richer) nearby Cotswold towns. All the houses and shops – apart from the eyesore of the modern police station – follow the original building line, the front doors leading straight off the street. Of stone, stucco, plaster and, occasionally, brick, some of the plain façades conceal interiors of great interest; many of the gardens retain the original burgage length, reaching nearly 200 feet to the old back lane.

46 High Street, on the corner of Gas Lane, is a prime example. Although its plain exterior, the stonework partly obscured by plaster, does not look promising, the inside provides a fascinating glimpse of domestic life more than 500 years ago. Here the building's structure shows clearly in the form of fine timber framing, which originally would have been infilled with wattle and daub – wickerwork covered with a mixture of horsehair and cow dung – the stone skin was added later.

A fine example of a mediaeval hall house, the rooms in number 46 are arranged to a simple plan in common use for several centuries. A central

Cricklade was still a quiet place in the mid-1920s. The war memorial had been built (behind the Crimean cannon) and John Pater's school had been extended in 1910.

passage divides the house, while on the left is a small room, low ceilinged and with a step down from the street level, which would have been a store or pantry. Above it was the solar, the only private area for the master and his wife. Almost all domestic activities would have taken place in the other, larger, room in which a huge fireplace was installed in the sixteenth century. Part of the fascination of this house is imagining how life was lived before that, when the hall would have been open right up to the roof with only a vent in the thatch to let out the smoke from the central fire. Today one of the most interesting things to see is the thick encrustation of soot on the roof timbers in the attic, the sight of which somehow brings home the reality of life so long ago.

The High Street shops and inns supply the people who live in the town and around it, and as such they do not exist to serve the antiques trade, or even take much account of passing tourists. Many of the old businesses and trades have disappeared; there are no drapers, cobblers, hat makers, tailors or saddlers any more, but their present-day replacements, whether grocer, newsagent, video shop or fast food outlet, no doubt serve the needs of the present-day population at least as well.

There were many more taverns and inns in the eighteenth and nineteenth centuries although the town seems well served now. The White Hart – mentioned as early as 1628 – and the White Horse were the main coaching inns, but the former took on a new role after the local hunt, the Vale of the

The funeral carriages of Clark Bros. who were the Cricklade undertakers and wheelwrights, photographed about 1900. The two brick-built houses behind the second carriage are now the town's post office.

Cricklade was well served with butchers' shops of which the best known was Carters, still a butcher's premises today. This is the Christmas Meat Show in 1901 although there are no turkeys hanging, only pig and sheep carcases. Mr. W.J. Carter is in the centre with his young son, W.M. Carter, behind him.

A variety of trades were represented in the High Street in the nineteenth century. The shop behind the Portwell pump later became the Medical Hall, and below was the wheelwright's; on the right was Golding, chemist and druggist, which was also the post office in the 1870s; next door was Goscombe the tailor.

It would be interesting to know what caused such a crowd to gather at the crossroads at a date some time after the clock was erected in 1897. Perhaps it was the arrival of one of the new-fangled motor cars that caused such excitement.

White Horse, was split into two 'countries' in 1886. New kennels for the VWH (Cricklade) were built on the edge of the town and the White Hart was rebuilt in 1890 to provide suitable superior accomodation for some of the hunting people who came to stay (and stable their horses) for part of the season. The White Horse, famous as an election headquarters for one or

Garfield House, newly built by the Postmaster, Mr. Harry Stephens, who also had a bakery there; the decorations were for the coronation of King Edward VII in August 1901. Mr. and Mrs. Stephens are in the doorway and their two daughters and a son-in-law are on the right.

The King's Head had acted as headquarters for one of the parties in the notorious series of Cricklade elections. On the right the children are coming out of Danvers House where the Misses Lovett and Miss Maslin ran a private school.

other candidate in earlier days, was not to be left behind and was renamed the Vale in an effort to attract some of this profitable business.

The large cast-iron clock standing at the main cross roads was paid for by public subscription (the Vicar making up the last few pounds) and was put up in 1897 to celebrate Queen Victoria's Diamond Jubilee. In a somewhat vulnerable position it has suffered several mishaps, but has survived as a useful and cheerfully painted piece of street furniture.

The buildings on either side of the narrow entrance to the Bath road had earlier been similarly buffeted, mainly by heavy waggons with their iron-shod wheels, and to protect them the Waylands feoffees placed some pieces of hard sarsen stones at the bottom of the corner walls. The origin of these stones, which are still in place (as is one at the end of Horsefair Lane), is somewhat mysterious, but the disappearance of stones belonging to what Aubrey described as a druidical temple at Broome was the subject of an inquiry in 1886, when it was reported that the Waylands trustees had purchased the remains of the temple and taken them to Cricklade for use in road repairs and maintenance!

The shop on the corner opposite the Vale was formerly the White Swan inn and was also a political headquarters – its landlord, Thomas Mann Gunn, bravely giving evidence in 1781 in Petrie's successful actions against the mass bribery which occurred in his inn and within his sight and hearing. Gunn continued to live in the town, although we have no record of how his testimony affected his relations with his customers or the Swan's profits.

A little further up the street is number 29, the red brick building that used to be Cricklade's post office. The Postmaster, Mr. Harry Stephens, had taken over the family bakery and corn dealing business from his father after spending some years in America, but the original shop burned down in 1896 to be replaced by much larger premises which he named Garfield House. He owned two other houses round the corner in Church Lane and also called them after American Presidents who had been assassinated whilst in office, McKinley and Lincoln; his granddaughter, Mrs Phyllis Hammond, followed the family tradition and called her home at Latton 'Kennedy'.

Some of the Saxon burgage holders in this upper part of the High Street were granted double widths of frontage, and it is here that the larger houses in the town are to be found. Danvers House, with its unusual Venetian windows, was for some time one of several private schools in the second half of the last century. The house was owned by the town's solicitor Joseph Lovett. Two of his daughters, Miss Jessie and Miss Lizzie, ran the school which was for both boys and girls, together with Miss Maslin.

Further up the street The Brow, a somewhat dour stone house, may have been built on the site of Garters Place, a property which figures in documents

Alkerton House was known as Pleydells for two centuries, called after the family who extended it and added the Georgian frontage. The earlier, Tudor, part (at right angles to the road) was behind the curtain wall, the columned porch being added later.

three centuries earlier and the site of which has never been identified for certain. Lloyds Bank was, before its adaptation for commercial purposes, a fine eighteenth-century house.

Next to the bank is the Alkerton Works where the business of Ockwells has continued the town's glove making tradition, making industrial gloves of many kinds. The building was, however, built for a very different purpose as it was to be the New Town Hall 'erected solely at the expense of Mr. J.W. Lansdown' and opened with a Grand Evening Concert on January 9th, 1862. The Lansdown family kept the White Horse (later to become the Vale) and Mr. J.W. Lansdown was, it seems, a capable singer. The *North Wilts. Herald's* account of the evening records his song 'King Christmas' as being sung 'very effectively and was rapturously redemanded', the report concluding: 'Mr. Lansdown must have felt much gratified at the reception both of himself and his concert, for the room was a bumper.'

Beyond, the Georgian frontage of Alkerton House disguises a much older Tudor building. The columned porch, described somewhat dismissively by the architectural historian Pevsner as being 'clumsy early nineteenth-century

Hunting played an important part in Cricklade life after the splitting of the Vale of the White Horse country into two in 1896. Beyond Alkerton House is the Town Hall; built in 1862 it later became a glove factory.

Mr. E.E. Giles of the Forty was the Cricklade milkman delivering both morning and evening; he grew prize dahlias and often wore one. Behind him is 23 High Street, in the garden of which a large cistern was placed in the eighteenth century to provide the first primitive water supply to part of the town.

Tuscan', was a later addition. Until the 1930s the house was known as Pleydells after the family name of its owners for some 170 years from 1605. The Pleydells were substantial local landowners, and Edward Pleydell's will and subsequent inventory dated 1632, gives in fine detail (for his property had to be meticulously divided between seventeen children) a comprehensive picture of the domestic possessions, farming tools, hunting equipment (cross bows, guns, fishing rods) and more personal items which such a large and well-off household would contain.

After the last of the Pleydells departed from Cricklade the property was used by various leaseholders for devious electoral purposes, and the next owner, Joseph Pitt, who came into the house when he purchased the Lordship of the Manor in 1815, continued this. Pitt, in financial difficulties, sold the property in 1834 to Dr. Thomas Taylor, the town's surgeon, who occupied the position of Bailiff (a title he changed to 'High Bailiff') for almost fifty years from 1827 to 1875. Dr. Taylor had a son, also a doctor, who became his partner and predeceased him by a year, and four daughters, the last of whom lived there until 1933 when the house, with its cottage, was sold for £1,325. The new owner was Mrs. Little, who had been born an Ockwell, and a little later the glove factory established itself in the old town hall next door.

23 High Street pictured about 1880. Although the date 1708 is over the door the architecture has the feeling of the William and Mary period rather than that of Queen Anne's reign, which began in 1702.

The Misses Taylor in the garden of Alkerton House about 1902 playing a game which was probably a ladies version of croquet, since the skirts of the period made it difficult to wield a mallet in the conventional manner! All four ladies remained unmarried, the last dying in 1933.

The Tudor part of the house lies at right angles to the street to the left of the porch, the gable end presenting a considerable problem to incorporate in the 'new' Georgian frontage. The solution was to continue the new façade but pierce new windows in the old gable end to make it look right, however inappropriate inside. The thickness of the Tudor chimney made it impossible to complete them all and that, and not the later window tax, accounts for the blank windows.

Architecturally the most distinguished building in Cricklade is the house opposite known simply as 23 High Street. With the date 1708 above its doorway it is an excellent example of a handsome town house built in the time of Queen Anne. Three interrelated families, the Tainters, Dennises and Byrts, owned the property throughout the seventeenth and eighteenth centuries; of these Morgan Byrt was the most notable.

Morgan Byrt, who was born in 1742, first became the town Bailiff at the age of 28 when he was described as 'yeoman'. Later on he was occasionally given the title of attorney although the qualification seems suspect. By 1790

An ox roast was held in Paul's Croft field to celebrate the coronation of George VI in 1937. Sir Percy Lawrie of the Manor House officiated; opposite him is Dr. Richards, the Vicar of St. Sampson's; the butchers were Mr. W.M. Carter (left) and Mr. W. Trinder, and on the extreme right was Mr. Fred Freeth, later to become High Bailiff.

when he became Bailiff for the second time he was 'gent. Captain of the Militia'; Morgan had certainly gone up in the world. He held the office of Bailiff more or less continuously until 1814, nine years before his death.

Byrt was implicated up to the neck in the electoral corruption of the time and there is no doubt that he used his triple position as Bailiff, parliamentary returning officer and head of the Waylands feoffees, to influence the allocation of leases of the Waylands properties. He had at his disposition many votes and used his power for the benefit of Lord Porchester. Called as a witness in the cases brought by Samuel Petrie in 1781 Byrt failed to impress the judge with his probity. 'Give a direct answer, you fence with every question that is put to you' he was told, and later pleading illness, which he referred to repeatedly, Petrie's counsel was forced to say that glad as he was he had recovered he only wished his memory had undergone a similar recovery.

Evasiveness, reprimands from the judge, outright lies, all mattered not a whit once he was home and the report of the Parliamentary debate which followed the trials concludes drily that 'the Bailiff of Cricklade continued in office'. Morgan Byrt lived on until 1823, when he died aged 81, unmarried and without legitimate issue, but still one of the chief citizens of the town.

Beyond number 23 the street slopes gently downhill, the houses and cottages on the west side still keeping to the building line against the

The largest house in Cricklade in the early years of the century was the Manor House in Calcutt Street, built in William and Mary style. An earlier house had been known as The Hermitage after a mediaeval hermitage believed to have been on the same site. Today it is Prior Park Preparatory School.

Mr. T. Butt Miller who was the Master of the VWH (Cricklade) hunt extended the already large Manor House in 1902. This picture, like many others in this book, was taken by Mr. W.G. Hayward, who had a tobacconist's shop in the town as well as being a very able photographer.

pavement which is considerably raised above the road. Opposite, and past Alkerton House and Cottage, the car park of the new Town Hall, erected in 1933, almost touches the line of the old town wall, the remains of which still lie under the grassy stretch by the road into Waylands. Until nearly the middle of this century there were no houses on this side of the road south of Alkerton Cottage and the old weighbridge, the field known as Paul's Croft being used for grazing.

The construction of the new road to Malmesbury (the B4040) effectively obliterated all traces of the town's station and the track bed was adapted for road traffic not long after the rails were lifted in the mid-1960s. Southwards, towards Purton, the high bank to one side is all that remains of the railway bridge.

The houses gradually tail off from here until at Dance Common the country begins again. It has only been a mile from the causeway and the High Bridge.

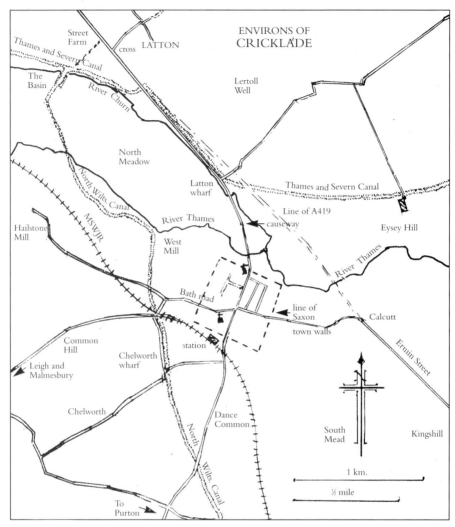

This composite map shows the road, railway and canals around Cricklade as they were during the second half of the nineteenth century. The places and features named relate to different periods of the town's history but all of them are mentioned in the course of this book.

CHAPTER EIGHT

Around and About and Near at Hand

There are places near to Cricklade which are within an easy walk, or a cycle ride of moderate distance, which are of great interest and well worth a visit. Here are some of them.

EYSEY AND WATER EATON

The gentle swell of Eysey Hill, topped by a rough growth of young trees and scrub and with the Thames curling round its base, is on the east side of Ermin Street as it passes Cricklade. For those with long memories it presents a somewhat nostalgic sight for Eysey church, St. Mary's, once stood there in its own churchyard now so sadly overgrown and neglected. The church itself is long gone.

Today, Eysey comprises just two farms, the Manor and Alex, with their associated cottages and buildings. The church registers, which go back to 1571, show that many more people must have lived there in previous centuries although the population steadily declined, resulting in the civil parish's amalgamation with Latton in 1897. Ecclesiastical union had occurred much earlier in 1819 and it may have been as a result of this that a mediaeval church which had stood atop the hill for centuries was demolished.

In 1838 Latton-cum-Eysey had acquired a new vicar, the Reverend Hyde Wyndham Beadon, who remained for fifty-three years. Perhaps it was he who urged the demolition of the simple four-square building at Eysey, nave, chancel and porch with gothic windows, shown in a drawing made about 1810, and its replacement in 1844 by a building typical of its time. A falling population meant declining congregations, and in 1953 this too was demolished to leave the hill bare but for its tangled churchyard.

Water Eaton, a scatter of farms and cottages along the road to Castle Eaton, is that part of Latton parish south of the Thames. At one time it had its own small chapel, St. Lawrence's, which came under the priest at Eysey; its site is thought to lie somewhere under the farm buildings of Water Eaton House. Little is known about it, but late in the last century tombstones were said to have been 'lying about in heaps' in the farmyard. Passage between the two across the Thames was by way of a series of large stepping stones, which as

The Victorian church at Eysey, consecrated in 1844, lasted just over a century before it too was demolished. There is no trace of it now and the gravestones lie in a tangle of undergrowth.

long ago as 1306 were said to be in existence 'of olde time'. It has been part of Castle Eaton ecclesiastical parish for many years.

LATTON

Latton, only a mile north of Cricklade along Ermin Street, has always kept its own identity and independence although so close to the town; the reasons for this are historic. Early on, Latton was on 'the wrong side of the river', for a time beyond the frontier which Cricklade defended. At the time of Domesday it was among the holdings of Rainbald, a priest of the Collegiate church at Cirencester which later became the Abbey. The dissolution of the monasteries in 1536 ended the Abbey's tenure and Latton was sold by the Crown to Sir Anthony Hungerford of Down Ampney. It has remained part of the Down Ampney estate of over 4,000 acres ever since.

The present owners, the Co-operative Wholesale Society, bought the estate in 1919. Whilst the number of people employed in agriculture and in the milk treatment plant (still familiarly, if inaccurately, known as 'the Creamery') is much reduced, at one time nearly all the houses and cottages were part of

The footbridge crossing the Thames on the path from Cricklade to Eysey; perhaps the curate had paused on his way to visit his parishioners. The fine elms are now all gone, casualties of Dutch elm disease in the 1960s.

the estate and almost everyone worked for it or for its tenant farmers. Many of the residential properties have since been sold to private ownership as the estate has been consolidated to be farmed as one unit.

Most of the village lies just off Ermin Street to the east where the church, St. John the Baptist's, stands on a raised site at a quiet crossroads. Much of the fabric is Norman, dating from around 1150 when the Abbey began to replace an earlier small chapel. The bottom stages of the tower are clearly of this period but it is the beautiful rounded dog-toothed arches of the period – to the doorway, and inside, to the tower and chancel – which confirm its age. Unhappily other traces of early work, ancient stained glass and some original fresco painting, disappeared in the wholesale restoration which was carried out in the 1840s and '50s.

The instigator of such radical changes was the new vicar, the Reverend Hyde Wyndham Beadon, mentioned above. The nave and transepts were subjected to what a directory of the time described in several successive issues

Ermin Street stretches towards Cricklade a mile away behind the waggon, traffic free in this nineteenth-century scene. Today, only the topmost step of the Cross, and part of the next, can be seen as the road level has become raised with successive resurfacing.

as 'progressive repair', although it may be only fair to point out that the chancel had already undergone a Gothic style enlargement only a few years before. However, Beadon cannot have approved of it for in 1859 a successful architect of the time, William Butterfield, was entrusted with further alterations. The bright, earthy colours of the patterned tiles used in the Sanctuary are a signature of his work.

There are few memorials on the walls and no old glass left in the windows, for most of these were replaced and dedicated to one or other member of the Beadon family. The Victorian glass, some of it in rather garish colours, is in striking contrast to the plain white walls and recently restored barrel ceiling.

The village road which ends just beyond the church turns into a footpath track leading into Down Ampney Park. It would have been by this route that the whole panoply of the court of Queen Elizabeth I would have passed on its way to enjoy the hospitality of Sir John Hungerford on September 1st, 1592; it would have been a bemusing sight for the simple villagers of the time.

The construction of the Thames and Severn Canal in the 1780s must also have been astonishing to the people of Latton, for 3½ miles of its length was within the parish – requiring the muscle power of hundreds of navvies to excavate and line the bed. The junction of the canal with the North Wilts. at Latton Basin is described elsewhere; it remains an interesting reminder of an era when water-borne traffic was practical and, for a time, economic.

Latton seems to have had a fairly stable population for at least 1,000 years. The detailed Domesday entry, with cottars, villeins and bordars listed, implies one of over a hundred. Even then it supported two mills on the Churn, both still working as late as 1773. The Lower Mill (near the Wharf) has since disappeared, but may well have taken on some of Cricklade's milling when the water supply to the Town Mill faltered.

THE LEIGH

Anyone who stops in Cricklade and asks for directions to Leigh and calls it 'lee' automatically declares himself a stranger. The village name is not only pronounced as 'lie' but given the prefix 'The' as well to confuse the unwary

St. Leonard's, Leigh, before most of it was moved to its new site in 1896. Today, the porch and doorway are on the south side of the nave, not as here on the opposite side. The sloping gates, or ones very like them, are still in place.

even more. The name derives from the Anglo-Saxon meaning 'a clearing in the forest where cattle can lie down'.

Most travellers only know The Leigh as the disparate collection of houses and cottages which straggle alongside the Cricklade to Malmesbury road soon after it has climbed over Common Hill. There is, however, much more to it and the loop of Swan Lane curving north from the main road has some agreeable farmhouses and a little known church of very great interest.

The *Shell Guide to Wiltshire* describes it as 'a small, bleak, late Victorian church' which perhaps only shows how the information printed in respected publications is not always reliable! In fact, almost all of it (the nave, tower and porch) was moved in 1896 to the place where it now sits, comfortable behind its wicket gates, from a site nearly a mile away. An earlier settlement at Waterhay, near the Thames, had gradually been abandoned and All Saints left on its own up a muddy track, surrounded by fields and apart from most of its parishioners.

The decision to move it was a bold one, not surprisingly opposed by the diocesan architect but, with the Archdeacon's encouragement and at a cost

The chancel (and nave wall) which were left behind on the original site at Waterhay, isolated in a field but tranquil in its peacefulness. An annual service is held here.

'not to exceed £1,300', it went ahead, each stone and piece of timber being carefully marked to correspond with drawings and ensure correct positioning. The chancel was left behind and remains on its original site, a serene place on a fine summer's day, the churchyard full of orchids and wild flowers. An annual service is held there although the structure is in the care of the Redundant Churches Fund.

The nave walls of this careful (and almost unbelievable) reconstruction are thirteenth-century but, on entering, it is the timbers of the roof, replaced in 1638, which amazes. Everywhere there are faces, animals, bosses, all intricately carved and of stunning variety in such an unexpected place. The beams and collars of the trusses are similarly carved and all combine to provide a worthy distraction – should one ever be needed – to a Sunday sermon.

BRADON FOREST

Mention 'Bradon Forest' to most people in and around Cricklade and their minds might well turn first to the comprehensive school in Purton which many local children attend. The name is apt, for the school draws its pupils from a wide area of north Wiltshire, much of which lay within the former boundaries of the huge royal forest of the same name. Nowadays only remnants of the woodland are left, a far cry from the time when John Aubrey, writing in the seventeenth century, could say that a squirrel (red, of course) could swing from bough to bough all the way from Wootton Bassett to Brinkworth churchyard.

Originally part of the vast forested area which covered much of southern England it was first mentioned in a Charter of 796. At the time of the Domesday survey it was estimated to cover about 15,000 acres but King John, a redoubtable hunter who came six times between 1200 and 1204, doubled the size. A few years after his death the first of several 'perambulations' took place in 1228 to establish the boundaries of the royal forest; today we would find the extent surprising for the boundary measured over 30 miles.

From Cricklade the line went southwards, following the course of the river Ray, past Lydiard Tregoze before turning west towards Wootton Bassett, close to Brinkworth then on to Garsdon before turning north past Charlton, going north of Minety before joining the Swill Brook flowing into the Thames, thence to Hailstone Hill, Cricklade. The former name of Hailstone Farm, Woodwards Farm, gives a clue to the prime task of its occupant.

Further perambulations followed, principally in 1278 and 1300, the boundaries constantly being readjusted as, owing to disafforestation, the forest was always contracting in size. Denuding the forest usually occurred as a result of local people using for their own purposes the resources that the king claimed as his own. There is no doubt that the people of Cricklade would have found the forest a fine source of timber for building and fuel and, after the land was cleared, it made good pannage for their pigs and grazing for their cattle. Although the forest reached the very edge of the town at the time of the first perambulation its boundary gradually shrank away, later perambulations showing that a wider band around the town had receded from the Ray to follow the river Key, south and west.

The nibbling away at the forest continued but it was not until 1611 that King James I decreed there should be heavy fines or corporal punishment (the one for the rich, the other for the poor) for pasturing cattle, lopping trees and taking firewood. The Commissioners charged with enforcing the decree apparently did little, as matters had probably gone too far, although two years later they were forced to report that the hunting would be poor because of 'the cattell there is no feed for the deer'.

James's son, Charles I, was firmer, however, and, short of money, he determined to resolve things to his own advantage if not that of the local people. In 1630 the Court of Exchequer declared Braydon to be 'the proper soyle of His Majesty and that he might enclose the same', all commoners' rights were to be extinguished and leases on the land would be sold. The three main purchasers were city of London merchants who just happened to be major creditors of the king; Philip Jacobsen, his court jeweller (said to be owed between £8,000 and £10,000), James Duart and Roger Nott, tailors.

A degree of uproar ensued and the 'quiet possession' promised by the king to the new owners was not achieved. Landmarks, hedges and rails were destroyed and there was a threatened attack on the Great Lodge (sadly now disappeared) where Jacobsen's agent lived.

Court proceedings rumbled on for years but in the end, since the commoners were unable to prove proper title to the land they had occupied, only a few concessions were gained. The chief ones were the grant of 150 acres for the extinguishment of small rights and a further 100 acres for 'the Second Poor of Cricklade', those whose sole livelihood would be lost if their former (illegally held) lands in the forest were enclosed. The Crown did not press its claim to the 212 acres of Common Hill, which remained commonland as it had been since before the Conquest. The rest was soon enclosed and divided up, the same boundaries defining the land of many of the farms which exist today.

Nowadays Bradon can still be a secret place. Open areas of farmland alternate with woods, many securely barred off from the road with strong wire mesh fencing. Secluded drives lead off to substantial private houses, many still called 'lodges' as a reminder of their former purpose – to provide lodging for the king and his lords during the hunt. Bradon Pond, at 39 acres the largest in Wiltshire, lies against the road but, fenced off, is inaccessible to even a casual walker. Public footpaths are few.

The forest of Bradon has always been hunted for deer rather than foxes. The practice must have continued in a less than natural manner for this 1884 picture shows a boxed stag being taken to its point of release before the hunt gives chase. On the right is the White Hart before it was rebuilt.

The big houses and farms apart, the dwellings (until recent years) provide a contrast to those in nearby villages. To the west and north, beyond the Thames, the Cotswold stone houses are larger and much more splendid. The forest houses very often speak of their origins as the humble dwellings of woodcutters or charcoal burners.

Another curiosity: there is no agreement on the spelling of the forest. To the Ordnance Survey it is Braydon; to the County Council who named the school it is Bradon; other writers refer to Braden.

Whichever way it is it hardly matters, for perhaps it is a part of the forest's mystery and considerable charm that its landscape is so near to Cricklade and yet so very different. The contrast adds to the pleasure that can be derived from a gentle exploration of this unspectacular but rewarding part of north Wiltshire.

Acknowledgements

Writing this book has been a pleasure and made me look anew at places I regarded as already familiar. As Editor of the publications of the Cricklade Historical Society I have been able to delve amongst its records and archives to obtain much of the material for the book; without such access I would have found writing it an uphill task.

The research carried out in the 1950s and '60s by the society's founder, the late Dr Theo Thomson (Cricklade's general practitioner as well as historian), provided me with much of the material for the early chapters. I am also particularly grateful to the curator of the Cricklade Museum, Tom Ramsden-Binks, for his patience in answering my many questions and allowing me to draw on his extensive knowledge of the town. For the chapter on Cricklade's railway I am indebted to the book written by the authority on the subject, Colin G. Maggs, *The Midland and South Western Junction Railway* (published by David & Charles).

The majority of the photographs have come from the Society's archive, and among them are many which I believe have not been previously published. I am also grateful to Mr. Jack Davey for loaning some of his extensive postcard collection, to Mr. A.V. Legg, and to others who offered photographs which I have been unable to use. Mrs. Phyllis Hammond's excellent memory has enabled me to add some details to the captions of photographs going back to the turn of the century.